The Complete Book of

AMERICAN TRIVIA

The Complete Book of AMERICAN TRIVIA

Jay Hyams and Kathy Smith

Rutledge Books
New York

To Wilhelmina Brookes
and Matthew and Nathaniel

Designed by: Allan Mogel
Edited by: Hedy Caplan

Library of Congress Cataloging in Publication Data

Hyams, Jay, 1949–
    The complete book of American trivia.

    1. United States—Miscellanea.   2. Curiosities and
wonders—United States.   I. Smith, Kathy, 1943–
II. Title
E156.H94 1983   973   83–11104
ISBN 0–87469–041–2

CONTENTS

Against the Law

The Puritans' blue laws weren't so named because they made people sad (although most of them seem to have been created for the express purpose of preventing people from having a good time); they are called blue laws because they were usually printed on blue paper.

The Puritans had very strict rules about conduct on the Sabbath (Sunday). It was against the law to cook food; shave or cut hair; travel (except to the meetinghouse); make beds; or sweep the house. Children were not allowed to play on Sunday; mothers were not permitted to kiss their children.

Puritan blue laws forbade sexual intercourse on the Sabbath. Since the Puritans believed that a child is born on the same day of the week it was conceived, parents of children born on Sunday were fined for having had sexual intercourse on the Sabbath (approximately nine months earlier).

The penalties for "breaking" the Sabbath were stiff: some transgressors were fined, and some suffered physical punishment, such as being put in the stocks. In 1656, a sea captain named Kemble was put in the stocks for two hours. His crime? Returning home after three long years at sea, he kissed his wife. He had committed this "lewd and unseemly behavior" on Sunday.

Respect for the Sabbath did not end with the Puritans. The king of Spain once asked Orville and Wilbur Wright to take him for a ride in their newfangled flying machine. The two brothers flatly refused—it was Sunday.

Upton Sinclair was once thrown in jail in Wilmington, Delaware, when he was caught playing tennis on Sunday.

During the 1880s, many towns in the Midwest had laws prohibiting the sale of ice-cream sodas on Sunday. Some owners of soda fountains found a simple and tasty way to please their customers without breaking the law. They left the carbonated water out of their sodas and served only the scoop of ice cream and the syrup. Thus was born the so-called Sunday soda, which has become the sundae.

In Topeka, Kansas, it is against the law for a waiter to serve wine in a teacup.

Puritan church services lasted upward of two hours, and there were fines for dozing off. To stay awake, many people took notes on the sermons.

Hawthorne's *The Scarlet Letter* has made the Puritan *A* for adultery famous. The Puritans used other letters for other vices: for example, *I* stood for incest and *D* for drunkenness.

Puritan Connecticut had very intricate laws regarding the smoking of tobacco. It was against the law for anyone under the age of 21 to smoke. People over 21 could smoke only if a doctor certified that tobacco contributed to their continued good health. These people had to get a special smoking license. With a license they were permitted to smoke—outdoors in open fields.

In 1638, Massachusetts passed America's first no-smoking ordinance. The law prohibited the smoking of tobacco outdoors and was not concerned with the smoker's health—it was to prevent fires.

In 1641, the Bay Colony of Massachusetts outlawed lawyers (the law was repealed, probably by a lawyer, in 1648). All lawyers were banned from the Colony of Virginia in 1658.

Games—any form of recreation—were illegal in many of the colonies, especially in New England. Idleness was against the law. Sir Thomas Dale discovered Jamestown colonists bowling in 1611 and promptly banned such frivolity. Massachusetts and Connecticut outlawed games, including bowling, dice, cards, shuffleboard, and dancing. Local law-enforcement officials were exhorted to search out singing, dancing, and game-playing. Performing a play in Connecticut earned the offender 15 lashes.

Well before 1700, cruelty to animals was a punishable crime in most of the colonies.

In 1700, there was a total of seven lawyers in New York City. Only three of these gentlemen had any legal training: one was a former maker of gloves; one was a dancing teacher; two were recent arrivals from England—where they had been whiling away their time in jail.

When the British soldiers who took part in the Boston Massacre (March 5, 1770) were tried for murder, they were defended by Josiah Quincy and John Adams (future second president of the United States). Adams did a good job—the British soldiers were acquitted (one had his thumb branded as punishment). Because of the strong anti-British sentiments in Boston, Adams lost more than half of his law practice.

The first chief justice of the United States, John Jay, bought slaves so that he could then free them.

F ollowing the Civil War, many young men didn't know what to do with their time. Some turned to outlawry. On Valentine's Day, 1866, Jesse and Frank James staged America's first daytime bank robbery. On October 6 of that year, John and Simeon Reno (the notorious "Reno Brothers") and a pal, Frank Sparks, pulled off the first robbery of a moving train. They rode away with over $45,000 but were soon caught.

In New York State, it is illegal to pawn an American flag; in several states, it is against the law to dance to "The Star-Spangled Banner."

In Colorado, it is against the law to pick wildflowers.

Al Capone, well-known gangster, carried a business card. According to his card, Capone was a "second-hand furniture dealer."

The original "ambulance chasers" were the lawyers of Howe & Hummell, a criminal-law firm in New York City during the 1890s.

The first woman prisoner executed in the United States was Mary Surratt, accused of complicity in the assassination of Abraham Lincoln.

Polygamy was outlawed in the United States in 1882 with the Edmunds Act.

The first execution by electrocution took place on August 6, 1890, at Auburn State Penitentiary, Auburn, New York. William Kemmler—who had hacked up his girlfriend with an ax—was executed.

Lizzie Borden was acquitted on June 20, 1893.

American Dishes

The weather for the 1904 St. Louis Louisiana Purchase Exposition was hot, and the oppressive heat led to the creation of a popular American food. Damascus-born chef Ernest A. Hamwi went to the exposition to sell a hot waf-flelike Persian pastry called zalabia. Next to his concession was an ice-cream stand. Because of the heat, Hamwi's hot zalabias weren't moving very fast, but the ice-cream vendor was selling so much ice cream that he finally ran out of cups. Hamwi got an idea. He took one of his zalabias and wrapped it around a scoop of ice cream. Christened the World's Fair Cornucopia, the new invention was quite a success—we call it the ice-cream cone.

The same heat that brought the ice-cream cone into existence caused problems for a young Englishman named Richard Blechynden. Blechynden had come to the exposition to sell good English tea—hot, of course. Few fairgoers were eager to slake their thirst with hot tea, and Blechynden was approaching despair. He dumped some crushed ice into an urn of tea, tasted it, and discovered it was quite delicious. Iced tea was born.

Dr. Thomas Bremwell Welch made his Dr. Welch's Un-fermented Wine for the use of local churches. The beverage was renamed Welch's Grape Juice and introduced at the 1893 Chicago World's Fair.

There were more Indians than Pilgrims at the first Thanksgiving celebration. The Indians brought with them a tasty snack that caught on with the English colonists: popcorn.

When Li Hung-Chang, Chinese ambassador to the United States, gave a dinner party for President Grover Cleveland on August 29, 1896, he decided to serve the president a completely new dish, something that would appeal to both Chinese and American tastes. He consulted with his resident Chinese chef, and the result was chop suey.

The average American dinner lasts 20 minutes—or less.

There was neither cranberry sauce nor pumpkin pie at the first Thanksgiving. What's worse, there weren't any forks. The only utensils were knives and spoons.

The Twin Popsicle was created during the Depression so that two children could share a Popsicle.

One evening at Moon's Lake Lodge in Saratoga Springs, New York, a guest complained about the french fried potatoes. Recently returned from a trip to Paris, the snobbish diner explained that in France french fries were much thinner and much tastier. A waiter dutifully removed the plate of chunky fries and brought it back to the kitchen, domain of head chef Chief George Crum. Although miffed, Crum sliced and cooked another batch of french fries and sent them out to the diner. Again the fries were rejected and again the waiter brought the plate back to the kitchen. The Adirondack chef sliced more potatoes, fried them, and sent them out—only to have them rejected again! Infuriated, the chef decided he had had enough. He sharpened a large knife, grabbed a nearby potato, and carefully cut it into transparent slices. He fried them up, threw them on a plate, and personally marched out of the kitchen and presented the plate of fries to the waiting customer. This time, they were not only thin enough—they were delicious! Indeed, they were the first potato chips. (They were known for a long time as Saratoga chips in honor of their birthplace.)

Lobsters were so plentiful in colonial Plymouth that they were considered fit food only for the poorest citizens, those unfortunates who could afford nothing better.

What's the most popular vegetable in the United States? French fried potatoes.

The Delicious apple was originally called the Hawkeye.

It was General Antonio Lopez de Santa Anna, the commander of the Mexican troops who stormed the Alamo, who introduced chewing gum to the United States. He was taken prisoner by Sam Houston at the Battle of Jacinto and brought to New York, where he met Thomas Adams of Jersey City. For reasons that remain unclear, Santa Anna brought with him a lump of chicle, the dried sap of the sapodilla tree. He suggested to Adams that it could be made into a kind of synthetic rubber. That idea failed, but Adams—who noticed that Santa Anna, like many Mexicans, delighted in chewing the chicle—found another use for the product: chewing gum. Adams's first gum was absolutely tasteless and was sold as Adams' New York Gum—Snapping and Stretching. One of the first flavors he tried was licorice, calling the product Black Jack. Black Jack is still on the market and is the oldest flavored gum. Remember the Alamo!

Baldwin apples were named for Lieutenant Colonel Loammi Baldwin of the 38th Infantry Regiment of the Continental Army, an officer who was with Washington on the evening of the Battle of Trenton.

Early American colonists ate apple pie with cheese for breakfast.

Pineapples are not native to Hawaii—they were first planted there in 1790.

Chili con carne was invented, around 1828, by Mexicans living in what is now Texas.

In the average American house, 788 cans of food are opened each year.

When, in 1921, the officials at Ellis Island immigration station in New York decided it would be nice to serve recent arrivals a truly "American" food, they began scooping out ice cream with every meal.

Early Americans ate a lot of corn. The method of softening the kernels was to soak them in water and lye, which made the kernels puff up when boiled and apparently didn't kill anyone.

When he passed away in 1921, at age 89, Hanson Crockett Gregory had had a long, full life. He had been one of Maine's youngest sea captains—he was given command of his own ship at age 19—and had seen the world. His greatest claim to fame, however, rests on something else. When he was just 15 and living with his family in Clam Cove (now Glen Cove), Maine, he stood one afternoon in the kitchen, watching his mother make fried dough cakes. After sampling one of the cakes, the youth complained to his mother, "Why doesn't the center cook up?" "They never do," she responded, frying more cakes. "They taste so soggy," lamented Gregory, his mind already working on the problem. Suddenly inspired, he took a fork and poked a hole through the center of one of the cakes—inventing the hole that defines the doughnut. There are other aspirants to the title "father of the doughnut hole," but Gregory seems the most likely candidate. Unfortunately, plans to erect a commemorative statue of Gregory, doughnut in hand, never reached fruition.

Colonials ate from wooden boards called trenchers. The food went in the hollowed-out middle. Some trenchers were double, for two people. Children were often fed at a separate table or were obliged to stand behind the adults and eat there in silence.

Americans eat 85% of their meals at home, and they eat 52% of those meals seated at the kitchen table.

Colonial children ate popped corn with cream and sugar for breakfast.

The cooks traveling with wagon trains going west did more than prepare the chow. The cook's last assignment at night was to point the chuck-wagon tongue at the North Star, providing a handy compass needle for determining the next day's direction of travel.

Half of the world's lemons are grown in the United States, mostly in California.

The first hot dogs were sold on Coney Island, New York, in 1871. Called dachshund sausages, they were sold without buns. Vendors handed the wurst to the buyer, who held it in his or her fingers. Some vendors supplied customers with white gloves to keep their fingers clean, but many customers "forgot" to return the gloves, making them an expensive addition to a hot-dog vendor's overhead. The problem was solved at the 1904 St. Louis Louisiana Purchase Exposition, when buns were introduced. In 1901,

Hearst sports cartoonist T. A. ("Tad") Dorgan went to the Polo Grounds in New York to make some sketches of a game. He playfully drew a picture of some barking dachshund sausages. Dorgan couldn't spell dachshund, so he labeled his drawings "hot dogs." The name stuck.

Delmonico's Restaurant in New York was one of America's first great restaurants and was wildly popular during the 1890s. Many items invented for the Delmonico menu have become American favorites. The creamed chicken dish called Chicken à la Keene on Delmonico's extensive—and expensive—menu was named for Foxhall Keene, the profligate son of a Wall Street financier. We now call the dish Chicken à la King. Lobster Newburg began as Lobster Wenberg, named for a regular at Delmonico's named Ben Wenberg.

American Revolution

The American colonies were not totally peaceful before the Revolution. Following is a list of some of the more important wars that took place in North America before 1775. Most of these are aspects of the ongoing struggle between England and France; the others are Indian wars.

Pequot War 1637
King Philip's War 1675–76
King William's War 1689–97
Queen Anne's War 1702–13
King George's War 1744–48
The French and Indian War 1755–63
Pontiac's Rebellion 1763–66

The first five American generals were Jedediah Prebel, Artemas Ward, Seth Pomeroy, John Thomas, and William Heath.

During the Revolution, the Continental Army suffered 4,435 battle deaths—342 navymen died; 49 marines.

Deborah Sampson was America's first female soldier. Aged 22, she took the name Robert Shurtleff and joined the 4th Massachusetts Regiment of Foot. She fought the British enemy on numerous occasions and was wounded at least twice—both times she refused treatment for her wounds in an effort to keep her secret.

In 1777, George Washington had every man in the Continental Army—about 4,000 all together—vaccinated.

The Battle of Bunker Hill was actually fought on Breed's Hill; the Battle of San Juan Hill was actually fought on Kettle Hill.

Benedict Arnold was a member of a Masonic lodge. The

lodge expunged Arnold's name when his coat turned out to be red.

Naval hero John Paul Jones ("I have not yet begun to fight!") had a hard time after his brilliant service during the American Revolution. He served in Catherine the Great's navy, fighting the Turks in the Black Sea, then went to Paris and died there during the tumult of the French Revolution, unknown and forgotten. In 1905, Horace E. Porter, ambassador to France, discovered Jones's grave after spending a great deal of his own time and money searching for it. In 1913, the hero's remains were enshrined in a crypt in Annapolis.

The American Revolution began on April 19, 1775, and George Washington proclaimed the cessation of hostilities on April 19, 1783 —a perfect eight years.

The Battle of Rhode Island, fought on August 29, 1778, is remarkable in that black soldiers fought against the British and Hessians. The blacks were slaves who had been freed for the emergency.

Only two American officers were wounded during the Battle of Trenton—one was future president James Monroe, shot in the shoulder by a Hessian.

At the age of 13, Andrew Jackson fought in the Revolutionary War. He was taken captive by the British at the Battle of Hanging Rock and was slashed with a saber when he refused to clean a British officer's boots.

Animals

Awolf may eat as much as 20 pounds of meat at a single feeding. Wolves only rarely attack human beings. The members of a wolf pack are most often related. The pack has two leaders, one male and one female. The leader of a wolf pack holds its tail straight out when walking. Other members of the pack let their tails droop.

No buffalo live in North America, and none ever have. The American buffalo is not a buffalo; it is a bison. Bison used to populate the East as well as the West, but the last one was routed in 1803.

In 1900, there were fewer than 30 bison left in the United States.

A female blue whale weighs as much as 30 elephants. A baby blue whale gains 200 pounds a day during its first year of life.

A flying squirrel can glide as far as 150 feet.

A bobcat is only about twice the size of a house cat.

Rodents gnaw things to keep their front teeth worn down; these teeth grow for the animals' entire lives.

The North American shrew has poisoned saliva and, relative

to its size, is one of the fiercest animals in the world. To keep up its energies, the shrew consumes its own weight in food daily.

Bears sometimes get cavities—from eating honey.

Smokey the Bear was real; he died in 1976. In 1950, he was found as a cub in Lincoln National Forest, New Mexico, orphaned and badly burned in a forest fire. Rehabilitated, he lived at the National Zoo in Washington, D.C.

Monkeys searching through their hair and their companions' hair are not looking for lice or fleas. They're searching for bits of loose, dead skin, which they eat.

A beaver can hold its breath for 15 minutes. Some beaver dams are as long as a football field and over 12 feet high.

The first lion in the United States was displayed to the public in Boston, Massachusetts, in 1716.

An earthworm that's cut in two doesn't turn into two worms. One section dies. The other part, if it hasn't lost too many segments, can stay alive and grow the missing segments back.

An armadillo can cross a river by holding its breath and walking across on the bottom. Only one of 20 different kinds of armadillos live in the United States—the nine-banded armadillo. It gives birth to four babies at a time, all of the same sex.

Bulls are color blind. They will charge anything waved in front of them.

The orca, or killer whale, is a type of porpoise.

Pigs will eat almost anything, but they won't overeat the way human pigs will. A pig can be taught to sit up or to roll over.

A dog often signals its intention to attack by holding its tail straight up.

The first dog-license law was established by New York State in 1894.

Elephants are not afraid of mice. Check it out at a zoo sometime—you'll see both together.

The horns of a bighorn sheep can weigh more than all the bones in its body—up to 30 pounds.

The desert cottontail and the brush rabbit can climb trees to escape enemies.

A male elk (bull) often fights to become the leader of a herd of females (cows). But he's then so busy fighting off challengers and keeping his females together, he gets exhausted and has to give up his leadership to a fresher bull after just a few weeks.

The front teeth of the North American porcupine are orange.

Most of the hundreds of thousands of pet gerbils in the United States are descended from nine Mongolian gerbils imported by a New York scientist for research in the 1950s.

A fox's tail keeps the animal steady as it runs.

A Rocky Mountain canary is a burro. Burros can recognize each other by the sound of their brays.

Newborn fawns have no scent, so enemies can't smell them.

The hairs of a moose's coat are hollow and give the animal buoyancy—moose are excellent swimmers.

Cats can't chew their food; they just cut through it and swallow.

The woodchuck, or groundhog, is a type of marmot.

Snakes smell with their tongues.

Horned toads are able to squirt blood from their eyes at their enemies.

Newts spend part of their lives on land, when they're called efts and have orange skin. When they turn back into water-dwelling newts they're green.

Crickets chirp rapidly on hot days but slowly on cool days. The rate of a cricket's chirping also varies according to the insect's age and state of health.

Worms get inside apples when female fruit flies deposit their eggs there.

Cockroaches coexisted with dinosaurs. Really think you can eradicate them?

A butterfly changes from a caterpillar inside a chrysalis; a moth metamorphoses inside a cocoon.

Some people aren't allergic to the mosquito's blood-thinning liquid; a mosquito bite doesn't itch them.

Bees may be induced to sting by the smell of some perfumes. It takes 1,000 bees' working lives to produce one pound of honey. A honeybee has two stomachs. One is to digest food and the other is to process nectar into a watery honey.

Assassinations

An attempt to assassinate Abraham Lincoln was made in 1861. It was foiled by Allan Pinkerton, the famous detective.

Andrew Jackson was the first president to suffer an attempted assassination. On January 30, 1835, an unbalanced painter named Richard Laurence shot at him with a pistol. When the pistol misfired, the man pulled out another one, aimed it at Jackson, and pulled the trigger. The second pistol also misfired, and Jackson attacked the assailant with his cane.

Robert F. Kennedy was the only presidential candidate ever assassinated.

In September of 1975, Gerald Ford suffered two assassination attempts. On the 5th of the month, Lynette Alice ("Squeaky") Fromme shot at him in Sacramento, California; on the 22nd, Sara Jane Moore tried to kill him in San Francisco.

Huey Long's assassin was Dr. Carl A. Weiss. Long was shot on September 8, 1935, and died on September 10.

Abraham Lincoln was wearing a Prince Albert coat, waistcoat, and trousers from Brooks Brothers when he was assassinated.

John Wilkes Booth was 26 when he murdered Lincoln.

Author, Author!

Hannah Adams (1755–1831), author of such works as *A Summary History of New England* and *The Truth and Excellence of the Christian Religion*, is considered the first professional woman author in America. She made very little money from her writing, however.

Louisa May Alcott, author of *Little Women*, was not particularly fond of children. She had a permanent writer's cramp in her thumb.

None of Horatio Alger's boy heroes ever became a millionaire—they did not really travel from "rags to riches." Rather, they merely bettered their lot in life. Alger was quite a prolific writer, turning out 119 novels in 30 years.

Sherwood Anderson, author of *Winesburg, Ohio*, died a very civilized, if tragic, death. He swallowed a toothpick with an hors d'oeuvre at a cocktail party and died of peritonitis and complications in 1941.

Upton Sinclair, author of *The Jungle*, ran for governor of California in 1934; Norman Mailer, author of *The Naked and the Dead*, ran for mayor of New York. Both men lost.

Richard Bach's *Jonathan Livingston Seagull* is the only book thus far to be the number-one best-selling American work of fiction two years in succession (1972 and 1973). The manuscript for the book was turned down by eighteen publishers before Macmillan finally decided to take a chance.

Herman Melville and Nathaniel Hawthorne were neighbors for a while in Massachusetts; Melville dedicated *Moby Dick* to Hawthorne.

Phineas T. Barnum published his autobiography, *Life*, in 1855 and kept revising it and republishing it for the next 35 years. He died in 1891.

Frank Baum, author of *The Wizard of Oz*, got the name of the magical kingdom of Oz from an alphabet card posted on the outside of a filing cabinet drawer—it read, "O–Z." Baum wrote 24 books for girls under the pseudonym Edith Van Dyne.

Ambrose Bierce was the first American author to use the word *gringo*.

Ambrose Bierce disappeared forever when he went to Mexico in 1914 to cover the revolution. No one knows what happened to him.

Augusta Jane Evans's novel *St. Elmo*, published in 1867, was so popular that towns in at least 13 states (Alabama, Tennessee, Georgia, California, Colorado, Illinois, Kentucky, Louisiana, Mississippi, Missouri, New York, Texas, and Virginia) were named for it.

F. Scott Fitzgerald was a notoriously poor speller.

The first woman newspaper editor in America was Ann Franklin, wife of James Franklin, brother of Benjamin. Her son, James, Jr., founded the Newport *Mercury*, and when he died, in 1762, she took over the paper.

Robert Frost, New England's poet laureate, was born in San Francisco. His father, a Southern sympathizer during the Civil War, named him after Robert E. Lee.

The masterful lawyer Perry Mason first appeared in *The Case of the Velvet Claws*, published in 1932 by Erle Stanley Gardner. Between 1933 and 1938, Gardner penned more than 1 million words a year—while still practicing law. He wrote 140 novels in that period, making him the world's fastest writer.

Zane Grey is the most filmed American writer—103 films have been made of his works. In 1936, Grey even made an appearance in a film: *The White Death*, an Australian-made film about a shark.

Bret Harte wrote verses for use in the advertisements of Sapolio, a laundry soap.

Nathaniel Hawthorne and Franklin Pierce were boyhood friends; they were together when Hawthorne died.

Ernest Hemingway was the first American wounded in Italy during World War I. (He was not a soldier.)

Robert Frost's epitaph reads: "I had a lover's quarrel with the world."

During the Spanish–American War, Stephen Crane (author of *The Red Badge of Courage*) got up early one morning and captured a town in Puerto Rico singlehandedly.

Bret Harte was fired from his job with a California newspaper when he complained too loudly about the massacre of a tribe of Indians at Humbolt Bay.

Ernest Hemingway rewrote the last page of A *Farewell to Arms* 39 times.

O. Henry is the pseudonym for William Sydney Porter. Mr. Porter wrote under the pseudonym for a very good reason (the same reason he gave out misleading information about his life and refused to allow his picture to be printed): he was trying to hide from the world, and especially from his daughter Margaret, the fact that he had a criminal record. He had served time in the Ohio Penitentiary for embezzlement of bank funds in Austin, Texas.

Ernest Hemingway wrote standing up; Mark Twain wrote lying down.

It was Edgar Allan Poe who created the genre called the detective story, the first being *Murders in the Rue Morgue* (in which the villain is an orangutan).

Washington Irving's last words were: "Well, I must arrange my pillows for another weary night! When will this end?"

Ernest Hemingway had a bit part in the film version of *The Old Man and the Sea*.

Sinclair Lewis was the first American to win the Nobel Prize (in 1930) for distinction in world literature.

Herman Melville based *Moby Dick* on a real whale named Mocha Dick. Mocha Dick was well known during the 1840s and 1850s, having caused the deaths of more than 30 men, sunk 5 ships, and survived 19 harpoons.

Edgar Allan Poe's epitaph is "Quoth the Raven never-more."

When he was an infant, Harold Robbins was abandoned on the doorstep of a Catholic orphanage in New York's Hell's Kitchen. The abandoned babe grew up to become the highest-paid, best-selling author in the world.

After the publication of *Uncle Tom's Cabin*, Harriet Beecher Stowe received a great deal of hate mail. One anonymous person sent her an envelope containing the severed ear of a slave.

Beginning in 1852, Harriet Beecher Stowe wrote almost one book each year.

Samuel Langhorne Clemens didn't invent the name Mark Twain (which means a depth of 2 fathoms, or 12 feet). It was first used by a riverboat captain named Isaiah Sellers, who used it to sign his column in the New Orleans *Picayune*.

In 1868, Mark Twain took part in the first chartered pleasure cruise, a trip to Europe and the Holy Land.

Mark Twain was born when Halley's comet appeared in 1835; he wanted to die when it was due to appear again, in 1910. He did.

Phillis Wheatley is considered the first important black woman poet in America. Born in Africa, she became the slave of a Boston merchant named John Wheatley. He encouraged her education and eventually freed her; she took her surname from him.

Gloria Steinem worked as a Playboy bunny to gather material for a story.

Harriet Beecher Stowe based the character of Uncle Tom on a real slave named Josiah Henson who was born in Maryland in 1789, escaped from Maryland to Canada, and became a Methodist preacher. He dictated his autobiography, *The Life of Josiah Henson*, in 1849; Stowe wrote the introduction to the book.

Mark Twain acted in a motion picture, *A Curious Dream* (1907).

Mark Twain was the first author to use a typewriter. He wrote *The Adventures of Tom Sawyer* on one, though he didn't want word to get around that he was using the machine—he was afraid he'd be asked to give testimonials.

Before *Uncle Tom's Cabin* was published, the best-selling novel in the United States was *Charlotte Temple*, by Susanna Haswell Rowson, published in 1792.

The term "It" for sex appeal—applied most famously to Clara Bow, the It Girl—was coined by novelist Elinor Glyn, a writer of what were considered at the time racy romances.

Hiroshima by John Hersey first appeared in the *New Yorker* magazine on August 31, 1946. It took up the entire issue.

A provision in Willa Cather's will (she died in 1947) prohibited publication of any of her works in paperback.

Birds

In 1810, almost one-third of all birds in the United States were passenger pigeons. The same year in Kentucky, ornithologist Alexander Wilson spotted a flock of the pigeons that was 250 miles long, made up of an estimated 2 billion birds. Another flock observed by John James Audubon, in 1913, flew by for three days. The last known passenger pigeon died at the Cincinnati Zoo on September 1, 1914.

The ring-neck pheasant is not native to the United States. It was brought here by hunters.

Cher Ami, a World War I hero, is stuffed and on display at the Smithsonian Institution. Cher was a carrier pigeon who flew through heavy fire to alert American forces to the presence of his "Lost Battalion" behind enemy lines. Cher Ami was recommended by General Pershing for the Distinguished Service Cross. He returned to the United States in a private stateroom on the *Leviathan*.

The U.S. Army disposed of its last homing pigeons in a public sale at Fort Monmouth, New Jersey, on March 23, 1957.

Early Mormon settlers in Utah faced starvation in May 1848 because of a plague of locusts. Seagulls saved the day on May 17 by devouring the pests.

Sparrows are not native to the skies of North America.

Eight pairs of sparrows were brought here in 1850 to eat caterpillars, but they found other food and thrived. Nor are the mice that plague our urban centers actually native Americans. The only mice native to the United States are the so-called field mice. Even honeybees—and their sting—had to be imported.

Lafayette brought the first partridges to the United States, in 1786, as a gift to George Washington.

Booze

The first beer brewed in the New World was brewed at Sir Walter Raleigh's Roanoke Colony in 1587.

In 1647, a certain Captain Brocas produced the first commercially successful wine in the New World.

The United States is the biggest beer producer in the world, making more beer every year than Great Britain and West Germany combined.

The oldest brewing company in the United States is D. G. Yuengling and Son of Pottsville, Pennsylvania, begun in 1829.

The Coors brewery is the biggest in the world.

During Prohibition, many breweries made milk. Coors made malted milk, some of which was used in the production of candy bars, like Mars and Milky Way.

The Manhattan cocktail, a concoction of whiskey and sweet vermouth, was invented by Jennie Jerome. Ms. Jerome, a New Yorker, married Lord Randolph Churchill, moved to England, and gave birth to Winston.

The martini was invented by Jerry Thomas, a bartender at the Occidental Hotel, San Francisco, in 1860.

The first beer sold in cans was Kreuger's Cream Ale, in 1935.

Budweiser was the first bottled beer sold nationally in the United States.

Between 1810 and 1830, the average American consumed

about 7 gallons of alcohol annually; in 1975, the consumption was down to 2.66 gallons.

Nevada has the highest per capita consumption of alcohol. Nevada consumes the most beer; Washington, D.C., the most hard liquor and wine.

Convinced that he was drinking too much, Buffalo Bill Cody decided to limit himself to one glass of bourbon a day and promised his friends he would stick to this intolerable limit. He suffered dearly, but he didn't want to go back on his word. He solved his problem by using a quart-size glass.

Boxing

The immortal line "We wuz robbed!" was uttered by Joe Jacobs, manager of Max Schmeling, at the end of the June 21, 1932, heavyweight title bout against Jack Sharkey.

Joe Louis grossed over $4 million as a fighter, but he never was a millionaire.

In an 1892 sparring exhibition, John L. Sullivan was knocked out by Hessie Donohue, his promoter's wife.

Sugar Ray Robinson's real name was Walker Smith.

The Joe Louis–Max Schmeling fight was broadcast on radio from ringside in English, German, Spanish, and Portuguese.

The last heavyweight championship fought bare-knuckled featured John L. Sullivan (the winner) and Jake Kilrain (the loser), who went an astonishing 75 rounds in Richburg, Mississippi.

Bridges, Buildings, and Sculpture

The statue of the president in the Lincoln Memorial was created by Daniel Chester French as an 8-foot-high sculpture. It was blown up to 19 feet by Attilio Piccirilli and his five brothers.

T he Waldorf-Astoria hotel in New York City owes its existence to a family feud. Mrs. William Backhouse Astor of Fifth Avenue was the leader of New York society in the early 1900s. Her nephew, William Waldorf Astor, was miffed that *his* wife wasn't the leader; he sold his mansion next to his aunt's so a hotel could be built there. It was called the Waldorf. Naturally, Mrs. Astor senior wouldn't live next door to a hotel, so she sold her property for a hotel named after *her*, the Astoria. United, they became the Waldorf-Astoria.

A B-25 bomber flew into the Empire State Building on July 28, 1945, striking the 78th and 79th floors.

The Verrazano Narrows bridge in New York City was designed by Othmar A. Ammans, a Swiss-American engineer. The bridge opened in 1964 as the world's largest single-span suspension bridge—60 feet longer than the Golden Gate.

The first hotel (as we know them) was the Tremont House in Boston. When it opened in October 1829, it offered, for the first time, private rooms, each with its own key (plus a bar of soap to use in the basement baths—private baths didn't appear until 1853).

The design for the White House, formally called the Executive Mansion, was the subject of an open competition, which was won by architect James Hoban. The building was finished in 1799, but was not called the White House until after it was burned by the British in the War of 1812 and painted white to cover the damage.

The log cabin was introduced to America by Swedish settlers in Delaware.

The first brick building in Boston was built in 1638.

Four women are represented in the U.S. Capitol's Statuary Hall. The sculptures are of Frances Willard, Maria Sanford, Florence Rena Sabin, and Esther Hobart Morris.

Lightning often strikes twice in the same place. In its first ten years, the top of the Empire State Building was struck 68 times.

New York's World Trade Center opened for business in 1972. At 1,350 feet, it was the world's tallest building until 1974. It is 100 feet higher than the Empire State Building.

Before 1957, high-rise buildings couldn't be built in Los Angeles. The building code was changed in that year, thanks to the development of earthquake-stress technology.

Self-service elevators (by Otis) were first used in the Atlantic Refining Building in Dallas, Texas.

The walls of the Arizona state capitol building are made out of tufa, a volcanic material.

The Empire State Building has 6,500 windows.

The Irving House, opened in New York City in 1844, was the first hotel to offer a bridal suite.

The Brooklyn Bridge, the world's first steel-wire suspension bridge, opened on May 24, 1883.

When the Ritz Carlton Hotel first opened in New York City, its rooms were equipped with bidets. The hotel was soon forced to remove them after suffering a deluge of complaints from outraged guests.

In the 43 years since it opened, over 600 people have jumped off the Golden Gate Bridge, an average of 14 suicides a year.

The tower of the Empire State Building was designed for the docking of dirigibles.

By Any Other Name

Being born with an awkward or thoroughly ordinary name is not necessarily an impediment to success as a performer—a name can easily be changed. Here is a list of extraordinary performers, who, unfortunately, were born with either ordinary or awkward names.

Eddie Albert (Edward Albert Heimberger)
Woody Allen (Allen Stewart Konigsberg)
Julie Andrews (Julia Wells)
Fred Astaire (Frederick Austerlitz)
Lauren Bacall (Betty Joan Perske)
Anne Bancroft (Annemarie Italiano)
Tony Bennett (Antonio Dominick Benedetto)
Robert Blake (Michael Gubitosi)
Charles Bronson (Charles Buchinsky)
Richard Burton (Richard Jenkins)
Eddie Cantor (Izzie Itskowitz)
Cher (Chereylynn La Piere)
Eric Clapton (Eric Clap)
Perry Como (Pierino Roland Como)
Alice Cooper (Vincent Damon Furnier)
Howard Cosell (Howard William Cohen)
Doris Day (Doris Von Kappelhoff)
James Dean (James Byron)
John Denver (Henry John Deutschendorf, Jr.)
Kirk Douglas (Issur Danielovitch Demsky)
Bob Dylan (Robert Zimmerman)
W. C. Fields (William Claude Dukenfield)
Ava Gardner (Lucy Johnson)
Judy Garland (Frances Gumm)
James Garner (James Baumgarner)
Samuel Goldwyn (Samuel Goldfish)
Elliott Gould (Elliott Goldstein)

Cary Grant (Archibald Leach)
Rita Hayworth (Margarita Cansino)
William Holden (William Franklin Beedle)
Boris Karloff (William Henry Pratt)
Jerry Lewis (Joey Levitch)
Hal Linden (Hal Lipshitz)
Dean Martin (Dino Crocetti)
Roy Rogers (Leonard Slye)
Suzanne Somers (Suzanne Mahoney)
Raquel Welch (Raquel Tejada)
Shelley Winters (Shirley Schrift)

Canvases

When John Trumbull set about painting *The Signing of the Declaration of Independence* (which can be seen on the back of any $2 bill), he wanted to accurately portray the signers. He was able to locate and paint from life 36 of them (this involved a lot of traveling: Jefferson was in Paris, John Adams was in London, the others were spread throughout the states). He copied 9 of the portraits from paintings by other artists, and he painted 2 of them from memory. He had particular trouble with the portrait of Benjamin Harrison. Harrison was dead, and he had never taken the time to sit for a portrait. Trumbull solved the problem by using a painting of Harrison's son. Everyone agreed that the son was the spit and image of his father.

Benjamin West's painting of the signing of the Peace of Paris, September 3, 1873—the treaty that ended the Revolution—is unfinished because the British representatives refused to pose.

Emanuel Leutze's famous painting of George Washington crossing the Delaware was painted in Düsseldorf, Germany. Leutze wanted to use real Americans as models for the soldiers, so he prevailed upon American tourists to sit for him. For the head of Washington, he copied the bust of him done by French sculptor Jean Antoine Houdin.

Clark Mills, a self-taught artist, made the first equestrian statue in America, a statue of General Jackson, done in 1853, for Lafayette Square, Washington, D.C. Mills had never seen either Jackson or any other equestrian statue. However, he did his job so well that Congress awarded him a bonus of $20,000 in addition to his original payment of $12,000.

The largest painting in the world is *The Battle of Gettysburg*, painted by French muralist Paul Philippoteaux. It took Philippoteaux and 16 assistants 2½ years to complete the painting, which they finally did in 1883. It is 410 feet long and 70 feet high and weighs 11,792 pounds.

The Museum of Modern Art in New York City hung Matisse's painting *Le Bateau* upside-down for 47 days before the error was discovered.

Cartoons

Bugs Bunny first said "What's up, doc?" in *A Wild Hare* (1939), the rabbit's fifth film appearance. The first Bugs Bunny cartoon was *Porky's Hare Hunt* (1937). The voice of both Porky and Bugs was Mel Blanc.

Daffy Duck was called "that darnfool duck" in his first film appearance, in *Porky's Duck Hunt* (1936). He became Daffy in his second film, *Daffy and Egghead* (1937).

The voices of the main characters on *Quick Draw McGraw* (Quick Draw, Baba Looey, Snooper and Blabber, Snagglepuss, and Augie Doggie) were all done by Daws Butler, except for Doggie Daddy, who was voiced by Doug Young. Butler also was the voice of Yogi Bear and Huckleberry Hound.

Mr. Magoo's first name is Quincy.

The Smurfs were created by Belgian cartoonist Peyo Culliford in 1957. There are 100 Smurfs; only one, Smurfette, is female. Their leader is Papa Smurf, who is 543 years old. Their enemy is the wicked wizard Gargamel.

The voice of Woody Woodpecker was provided by Walter Lantz's wife, Grace Lantz.

The first Road Runner–Wile E. Coyote film was *Fast and Furry-ous* (1948). The Road Runner's only words were "Beep beep!" Wile E. Coyote spoke just once, in *Operation Rabbit* (1951), a Bugs Bunny cartoon.

The Flintstones live at 345 Stone Cave Road in Bedrock. Fred works for the Slaterock Gravel Company. He and Barney Rubble belong to The Royal Order of Water Buffalos. It all takes place in the one million forties B.C.

Chiefs of State

Dwight D. Eisenhower played football while he was a West Point cadet. He hurt his knee during one game when he tried to tackle Jim Thorpe. (It may be that Thorpe was wearing the sheet-metal shoulder pads he was famous for.)

Many presidents have been passionate golfers, but only Eisenhower and Ford made holes in one.

Ronald Reagan served as a lifeguard while in high school. He saved 77 people from drowning.

The third son of Benjamin Harrison, patriot and signer of the Declaration of Independence, was named William Henry. William Henry Harrison became the ninth president of the United States. He and his wife had ten children, the most of any presidential couple. Only one of these children survived its mother, but that one had a son named Benjamin—and Benjamin became the twenty-third president of the United States.

Chicago has been the scene of more presidential nominations than any other city, with a total of 10.

The planet (asteroid) Hooveria was named for Herbert Hoover. The planet was discovered in 1920 by Johann Palisan of the University of Vienna. He named it in honor of Hoover, who was not yet president but was popular with Europeans because he was chairman of the commission bringing food and clothing to the people of war-devastated Europe.

Christmas at the White House: Dwight and Mamie Eisenhower sent out 1,300 Christmas cards; John and Jackie Kennedy mailed 2,300; LBJ and Lady Bird sent 30,000; Dick and Pat Nixon greeted 60,000 friends; the Fords, Jerry and Betty, sent 45,000 cards; Jimmy and Rosalyn Carter sent 60,000.

George Washington died on the last hour of the last day of the last week of the last month of the last year of the eighteenth century.

John Adams was the longest-lived president yet, living to be 90 years and 247 days old.

James Madison was the last of the Founding Fathers to die. He was the last signer of the Constitution; the last of the Continental Congress; and the last of the Virginia Constitutional Convention of 1776.

William Henry Harrison's term as president was the shortest: March 4, 1841 to April 4, 1841.

Grover Cleveland was both the twenty-second and twenty-fourth president, the only president to serve two nonconsecutive terms.

To date, Franklin Pierce is the only president to maintain his cabinet intact for an entire administration.

Zachary Taylor never voted in a presidential election.

John Tyler, the tenth president, was a delegate to the Provisional Congress of the Confederate States of America and was elected to the House of Representatives of the Confederate Congress. He died before taking his seat, and it is not surprising that no official mention was made of his death.

Dwight D. Eisenhower used Franklin Roosevelt's retreat in the Maryland mountains for special meetings and entertaining official guests. He changed the name, however. Roosevelt had called the place Shangri-la; Eisenhower named it Camp David.

Ulysses S. Grant laid the cornerstone for the American Museum of Natural History on June 2, 1874.

Rutherford B. Hayes was wounded while serving as a Union officer during the Civil War.

When William Henry Harrison died one month after his inauguration as president, John Tyler, vice president, was in Williamsburg, Virginia. It took a long time to track him down and inform him of the president's death. When Tyler finally reached Washington, D.C., the nation had gone 53 hours without a president—the longest such period thus far.

What did George Washington want to be when he grew up? Like many boys in the British Empire, he dreamed of becoming an officer in the Royal Navy.

Tireless Teddy Roosevelt was an avid reader. On a trip through the jungles of Brazil, he spent his evenings reading Gibbon's *Decline and Fall of the Roman Empire*; while part of a posse tracking down a gang of outlaws through the Dakota badlands, he read *Anna Karenina*.

Stephen A. Douglas and Abraham Lincoln both sought the hand of Mary Todd. When Mary chose Lincoln as her suitor, it did nothing to diminish Douglas's dislike of him.

Herbert Hoover was a member of Stanford University's first graduating class.

In 1805, Thomas Jefferson offered Lafayette the governorship of Louisiana. The French hero refused.

In 1868, the American Colonization Society was formed to establish a colony in Africa to which 200,000 blacks—freed or born to free parents—could be sent. In all, about 15,000 blacks left America for the colony, which came to be called Liberia. The capital city of Liberia is Monrovia, named for James Monroe—the only foreign capital named for an American president.

John F. Kennedy had illegible handwriting.

Thomas Jefferson was never a member of any church.

Sigmund Freud felt that Woodrow Wilson had a Messianic complex.

Although his birthplace is officially given as Fairfield, Vermont, Chester A. Arthur may have been born in Canada.

Martin Van Buren, born in 1782, was the first president born after the American Revolution, hence, the first president born a citizen of the United States rather than an English colonist.

In December of 1857, Ulysses S. Grant, future president of the United States, found himself in such poor financial straits that he was forced to pawn his watch. He got $22 for it—just in time for Christmas.

Lincoln did not want to go to the theater on April 14, 1865. He had already seen the play, *Our American Cousin*, and was not anxious to see it again.

Cities

The population of Columbia, South Carolina, has the highest proportion of unmarried males: 57.1%; Brookline, Massachusetts, has the highest proportion of unmarried women: 59.6%.

New York City leads the nation in reported sightings of ghosts.

The United States has 27 cities with over 1 million inhabitants—more than any other nation, even China.

New York City's population is larger than that of a number of countries, including Denmark, Austria, Norway, and Switzerland.

Albany received its charter in 1686 and is the oldest chartered city in the United States.

Harlem was the first, and only, place in New York City where blacks could find good housing when it was originally developed in 1901. It didn't become a ghetto until the 1920s.

The dead are buried aboveground in New Orleans because the local ground is too damp for interment.

Large cities are the birthplaces of only two presidents of the United States: New York City—Theodore Roosevelt; and Cincinnati, Ohio—William H. Taft.

The first American city to have a zoo was Philadelphia. It opened in 1874.

The city of New York was begun in 1612 when two Dutch ships arrived in the Hudson River to trade with the local

Indians. Huts were put up on the island to store trade goods. The probable location of the huts is 45 Broadway.

It would take a log thrown in the Hudson River at Albany, New York, more than a year to reach the Atlantic Ocean.

The Watts and Newark ghetto riots of the 1960s began over disputes about traffic tickets.

The East River Drive in New York City was constructed on unusual fill—rubble from the World War II air raids on London; it was a gift from the British government.

Cincinnati was the first American city to have a modern, salaried fire department; it was also the first city to issue each man a fire hat, in 1851.

Almost all early visitors to Manhattan Island commented on the sweet-smelling grasses and wildflowers growing abundantly on the island. The waters of the Hudson River were so sweet that the Dutch settlers preferred drinking the water to beer.

The first baptism in America took place, in 1540, along the Acuulgee River, near what is now Macon, Georgia. An Indian guide was baptized by priests from De Soto's retinue.

The capital city of Texas was changed 15 times—it's a big state—before Austin was finally settled on.

The most severe earthquake to hit the United States was not the San Francisco quake of 1906 (8.25 on the Richter Scale), but the Alaskan quake of 1964 (8.4). The quake flattened all of Anchorage's downtown business section.

Boston Public Garden's famous Swan Boats debuted in 1877. They were designed by Robert Paget.

The city of Brooklyn merged with the city of New York on January 1, 1898.

The average annual snowfall in Buffalo, New York, is 88.6 inches, the highest in the United States. Phoenix, Arizona, gets the most sun; Miami, Florida, gets the most rain.

Houston and Honolulu are the warmest of the 50 largest American cities. They have average temperatures of 76.1 degrees.

Santa Fe, New Mexico, receives an average of 17 more inches of snow than Fairbanks, Alaska.

The average winter temperature in Reykjavik, Iceland, is higher than the temperature in Chicago, Illinois.

There are 23 yards of "green" space (area in which to move about) per inhabitant of New York City; in Tokyo there is 1 yard; in Oslo there are 340.

Civil War

The first shot of the Civil War was fired at Fort Sumter at 4:30 a.m., April 12, 1861. The honor of pulling the lanyard that fired the shot went to Edmund Ruffin, an avid secessionist. Ruffin lived through the war years and committed suicide when he learned of Lee's surrender.

The shot fired by Ruffin hurtled across the water and slammed into a wall of Fort Sumter at a point near the right ear of Captain Abner Doubleday, the man officially honored as the creator of baseball at Cooperstown, New York, in 1839.

The commander of the Confederate soldiers firing at Fort Sumter was General P. T. Beauregard; the commander of the Union forces in the fort was Major Robert Anderson. The two men knew each other well: Anderson taught artillery at West Point, and Beauregard had been one of his star pupils.

At the beginning of the Civil War, Robert E. Lee was offered command of the Union Army; William T. Sherman was offered an important high command in the Confederate army.

During the Civil War, the Union Army lost more men to disease than to enemy bullets.

The First Battle of Bull Run (also called First Manassas), July 21, 1861, was not the first battle of the Civil War—it was preceded by a month by Big Bethel.

The Civil War was expected to be a short, glorious affair, and the soldiers of the First New York Regiment marched off toward Bull Run wearing uniforms from Brooks Brothers and carrying sandwiches from Delmonico's.

Jefferson Davis, president of the Confederate States of America, served as secretary of war under Franklin Pierce. In that office, he had approved the appointment of George Armstrong Custer to West Point. It was Custer, golden locks bouncing, who rode out to accept the surrender of Lee's forces, taking into his own hands the white linen towel used by Lee's emissary to set up the surrender meeting. (Eleven years later, this same Custer rode forth to another kind of fame at the Little Big Horn.)

The Civil War was a very personal affair for Wilmer McLean. In 1861, he had a nice farm spread along the banks of the Bull Run, near Manassas Junction, Virginia. The first big battle of the war took place in his frontyard; one of the first cannon shots of the battle went through his kitchen. Deciding that he wanted no more of the war, McLean moved to a quiet town south of Richmond, Virginia, a town named Appomattox Courthouse. The surrender of Lee's army took place in McLean's living room, on April 9, 1865. Officers from both armies tore his furnishings apart for souvenirs.

Robert E. Lee saw his first combat action of the Civil War at the Battle of Cheat Mountain, February 15, 1861.

At the age of 21, Henry M. Stanley enlisted in the Sixth Arkansas. Stanley fought for the South until he was taken prisoner; he then changed uniforms and fought for the North. The Welsh-born adventurer survived the war and, on November 10, 1871, after 11 months of searching through the wilds of Africa, made headlines by saying, "Dr.

Livingstone, I presume." David Livingstone, the Scottish missionary and explorer of Africa, found by the tireless reporter, had not been untouched by the Civil War. His son, aged 18, had been killed while fighting in a Massachusetts regiment at Gettysburg.

George Gordon Meade, commander of the Union forces at Gettysburg, was born in Spain of American parents.

The first—and thus far only—woman to win the Congressional Medal of Honor was Dr. Mary Edwards Walker, who was honored for her service as a doctor during the Civil War. An ardent feminist, Walker assumed male attire in civilian life and was once arrested in New York for "masquerading as a man." She was also an enemy of tobacco. In 1917, the government tried to revoke her medal, but she refused to give it back and wore it every day—she was buried with it.

"The Civil War" is only one of the many names for the conflict that raged from 1861 to 1865. Among the Civil War's other names are:

The War Between the States
The War Against Northern Aggression
The War for the Union
The Great Rebellion
The Second American War of Independence
The War for Separation
The War for Abolition
Mr. Lincoln's War
The War for States' Rights
The War for Southern Independence

On the staff of Confederate cavalry leader Jeb Stuart was Major H. B. McClellan, first cousin of George B. McClellan, Union general.

One of the soldiers killed at the bloody battle of Shiloh was a man who had seen action on another famous battlefield. Hugh McVey, an Irishman fighting for the South, was 70 years old when he was killed; at age 25 he had fought at Waterloo.

Confederate general Nathan Bedford Forrest had 29 horses shot from under him. He survived the war to become a founder of the Ku Klux Klan.

The Civil War divided many families. Henry Clay had seven grandsons: three served the Union, four the Confederacy.

Arthur MacArthur enlisted in the Union Army at age 17, fought bravely in many battles, and was awarded the Medal of Honor. His son had a lot to live up to—General Douglas MacArthur did his best.

Many battles of the Civil War are known by two names, the name given the battle by the Union Army and the name given by the Confederate Army. Among the battles with two names are:

UNION	CONFEDERATE
Bull Run	Manassas
Antietam	Sharpsburg
Fair Oaks	Seven Pines
Stones River	Mufreesboro
Elkhorn Tavern	Pea Ridge
Shiloh	Pittsburg Landing

Robert E. Lee was a small man. His shoe size was 4½.

During the summer of 1864, Confederate general Jubal A. Early reached the outskirts of Washington and threatened to attack the capital. Abraham Lincoln went out to get a look at the battle, and the tall man in the black suit and stovepipe hat immediately became a popular target for Rebel sharpshooters. Even with the minié balls whistling by his ears, Lincoln continued to stand at the ramparts until a captain near him screamed, "Get down, you damn fool, before you get killed!" Lincoln turned to the young officer and said, "Well, Captain, I see you have already learned how to address a civilian." The young captain was Oliver Wendell Holmes, Jr.

Many future presidents took part in the Civil War, including Rutherford B. Hayes, William McKinley, Ulysses S. Grant, Chester A. Arthur, James A. Garfield, and Benjamin Harrison. Confederate general John C. Breckinridge had served as vice president of the United States under Buchanan.

The Civil War ended on Palm Sunday, April 9, 1865.

The final battle of the Civil War took place in the Bering Straits, where the Rebel raiding ship *Shenandoah* came upon some Yankee whaling ships. It was June 28, 1865—the war had officially ended that April.

The last participant of the Civil War to die was Walter Williams, who died at age 117 on December 19, 1959. He had served with the South.

Columbus

The member of Columbus's crew who first sighted land on October 11, 1492, was Roderigo de Triana, aboard the *Niña*. The land sighted, called San Salvador by Columbus, is probably Watling Island. Columbus asked for, and was given, the reward for sighting land that should have gone to de Triana.

Christopher Columbus had white hair when he arrived in the New World. He was 41 years old.

Columbus never even saw—let alone landed on—any part of the present United States.

Most educated people in Columbus's time believed that the earth was round.

Columbus did not allow his sailors to swear.

Christopher Columbus never realized that he had not reached China. He died, in 1506, blissfully certain that he had reached Asia.

Comestibles

Oscar Tschirky, maitre d' of the Waldorf-Astoria's restaurant when it opened in 1893, is famous for inventing the Waldorf Salad (a concoction including diced apples, celery, nuts, and mayonnaise). Mr. Tschirky is also responsible for a creation less pleasing to hungry restaurant patrons—he installed the first plush rope behind which customers had to wait for a vacant table.

Diamond Jim Brady may be America's most famous "gourmand" (*glutton* would be a better word). He ate six meals a day, and at each meal he devoured more than enough food to stuff a very large family. For dinner, he was fond of eating two or three dozen oysters; a half dozen crabs; seven lobsters; a double portion of terrapin; two ducks; a large sirloin steak; and two pounds of chocolates. Nearly as offensive as the quantities of food he consumed was his choice of beverage. Diamond Jim washed all this expensive restaurant fare down with orange juice or lemon soda pop.

Parkerhouse rolls are named for a restaurant in Boston called the Parker House.

The first credit-card company was the Diners' Club, begun in 1950.

America's first pizzeria opened on Spring Street in New York City in 1895.

Jewish immigrants coming to the United States during the late 1880s brought along food to eat on the long sea voyage, including hunks of their own kosher dried beef. They would scrape off some meat, mix in a little chopped onion, and form the combination into little cakes. These patties came to be called Hamburg steaks, named for the beef, from the German city of Hamburg, of which most were composed.

Yale College in New Haven, Connecticut, served apple pie for dessert at supper every night for more than 100 years.

By law, the Congressional cafeteria in Washington, D.C., must have Yankee Bean soup on the menu every day. This law is attributed to Joseph Gurney Cannon, speaker of the House (1903–11), known for carrying the power of his office to arbitrary extremes. According to tradition, he happened to come into the cafeteria on a day when Yankee Bean soup was not on the menu, and he determined that it should never happen again.

Catsup was first sold in this country as a kind of patent medicine. One popular brand during the 1830s was Dr. Miles's Compound Extract of Tomato.

Every American farmer grows enough food to feed himself, 45 other Americans, and 8 foreigners.

Thomas Jefferson introduced french fries to America. He encountered them while serving as ambassador to France. He also started the habit of eating steak and french fries.

Tollhouse cookies are named for the Toll House Inn in Whitman, Massachusetts, where they were invented by a certain Mrs. Ruth Wakefield. While mixing up a batch of Butter-Drop Do cookies, she decided it might be nice to add some chopped-up chocolate bits. She thought the bits of chocolate would melt; they didn't, and she was delighted with the result.

Americans eat an average of 245 pounds of meat every year, which is more than any other nationality (second are Argentines; Australians are third).

The average American supermarket stocks 12,341 items.

The residents of North Carolina consume more soft drinks per person than any other state.

Comics

Rube Goldberg drew a Sunday comic strip for 20 years called "Boob McNutt." It featured Boob; his girl friend (later wife) Pearl; their Siberian cheesehound, Bertha; and the twins Mike and Ike ("I'm Mike," "I'm Ike," they said).

The first American comic strip to gain an international following was "Bringing Up Father," by George McManus, which debuted in 1913. Jiggs and Maggie got their money by winning the Irish Sweepstakes. Before that, Jiggs was a mason and Maggie, a washerwoman.

"Mutt and Jeff" started as "A. Mutt" in 1907, the first daily comic strip. Mutt met Jeff in 1908. Jeff was named after boxer Jim Jeffries. The strip was drawn by Bud Fisher until his death in 1954, when artist Al Smith took over.

"Barnaby" was drawn by Crockett Johnson from 1942 until 1946 and continued until 1954. Its child hero had a dog named Gorgon (who talked, but not in front of grownups) and three odd friends—Lancelot McSnoyd, an unpleasant goblin; Gus, a timid ghost; and Mr. O'Malley, a leprechaun.

The creator of Wonder Woman, William Moulton Marston (pseudonym Charles Moulton), was a psychologist who also invented the polygraph.

The predecessor of "Polly and Her Pals" (which ran for 40 years from its debut on December 4, 1912) was "For This We Have Daughters?" and featured the same basic four characters. "For This" became "Positive Polly," which became "Polly and Her Pals." The Sunday feature started as "Here, Gentlemen, Is Polly!" which became "Polly!" then "Polly," and finally "Polly and Her Pals."

Al Capp originally signed himself as Al G. Cap—both being abbreviations of his full name, Alfred Gerald Caplin. "Li'l Abner" first appeared in 1934. Before drawing the denizens of Dogpatch (which is in Kentucky), Capp was an unsigned artist for "Joe Palooka," by Ham Fisher.

Captain Marvel's appearance was inspired by Fred MacMurray. *Shazam* stands for *Solomon's* wisdom, *Hercules's* strength, *Atlas's* stamina, *Zeus's* power, *Achilles'* courage, and *Mercury's* speed.

"Rex Morgan, M.D." (debut: 1948), "Judge Parker" (1952), and "Apartment 3-G" (1961) were all originated by Dal Curtis (Nicholas Dallis), a cartoonist and psychiatrist.

Cartoonist Dave Breger created the cartoon "G. I. Joe" for *Yank* magazine; it first appeared on June 17, 1942, and within a week Breger's coined term had swept the country.

For many years the "Buck Rogers" Sunday feature didn't feature Buck Rogers. Instead it starred Bud Deering (Buck's girl friend Wilma's younger brother) and *his* girl friend, the Martian princess Alura.

Katzenjammer means "hangover" in German. Its literal meaning is "the yowling of cats." The "Katzenjammer kids" introduced the word *nix* to the English language, an Americanization of *nichts*, German for "nothing." The Kids were the first cartoon characters to talk in the now-familiar balloons.

"Krazy Kat" started in 1911 and ran until 1945. Drawn by George Herriman, it featured Krazy, Ignatz the Mouse (who threw bricks), and Offissa B. Pupp. Minor characters included Joe Bark, Don Koyote, Mock Duck, Kristopher Kamel, Bill Bee the Bum, and Alec Katt.

Charles Schulz was a cartoonist for the St. Paul *Pioneer Press* when he began "Peanuts."

"Doonesbury" began as "Bull Tales" in the *Yale Daily News* in 1969. It was syndicated in 1970.

Mad magazine developed from *Mad* comic book, first marketed in August 1952. Alfred E. Neuman's original name, Melvin Cowznofski, was given to him by comedian Ernie Kovaks.

Etta Kett is a takeoff on the word *etiquette*, which the strip was supposed to teach teenagers when it first appeared in 1925.

Flip Corkin in "Terry and the Pirates" was based on cartoonist Milton Caniff's friend Captain Philip G. Cochran of the U.S. armed forces.

Comic-Strip Characters

Mary Worth originated during the Depression as Apple Mary. She was plumper and more dowdy in those days than she is now, but even then she kept busy by solving other people's problems.

Spider-Man debuted in *Amazing Fantasy* (Marvel), no. 15, August 1962.

Barney Google's race horse was named Spark Plug, his girl friend was Sweet Mama, and his pet ostrich was Rudy. Snuffy Smith joined Barney in 1934 and gradually took over the strip.

When the New York papers went on strike in 1937, Mayor Fiorello H. LaGuardia read the comic strips over the radio so the city's kids (and adults) wouldn't miss them.

The hero of "Skippy" was 10-year-old Skippy Skinner, whose friends were Sooky Wayne and Sidney Saunders.

Smilin' Jack and his wife, Joy (who periodically vanished), had a son, Jungle Jolly.

Alley Oop lived in the Stone Age Kingdom of Moo with, among others, his girl friend, Oola, and King Guzzle I.

Tillie the Toiler's boyfriend was Clarence MacDougall, called Mac, whom she finally married in April 1959 (Tillie debuted in 1921—an over-long courtship).

Mandrake the Magician's opponent was The Cobra, another magician.

Melissa, the elderly patient and fixture in "Rex Morgan, M.D.," has no last name.

Before Daddy Warbucks entered the scene (incidentally, he was a munitions manufacturer), Little Orphan Annie's closest friend—in addition to Sandy—was her doll, Emily Marie.

One of World War II's most popular pinups was Miss Lace, the heroine of "Male Call," a strip drawn by Milton Caniff without pay for G.I.s at the same time he was being well-paid for "Terry and the Pirates."

The Hulk was originally gray.

The Human Torch was created as an android by Professor Horton, who was later accidentally killed by the Torch.

Batman was originally called Birdman by his creator, Robert Kane. By the time the Caped Crusader debuted in *Detective Comics*, in 1939, he had acquired his new name. He wore a pair of wings at first.

Brenda Starr, *Flash* reporter, debuted in 1940, met Basil St. John—the "mystery man"—in 1945, and married him in 1975.

When she debuted in 1930, Blondie Boopadoop was a flapper and her future husband Dagwood was a playboy. Dagwood was disinherited by his railroad magnate father when he and Blondie were married on February 17, 1933.

Before acquiring his astonishing powers, Plastic Man, the vain superhero in shades, was Eel O'Brien, a petty thief. His sidekick, Woozy Winks, was a jail-breaker.

Happy Hooligan wore a red can for a hat; originally, the can was blue.

Skeezix was left on Uncle Walt Wallet's doorstep on Valentine's Day, 1921.

Bathless Groggins appeared in "Abbie an' Slats"; he was the father of Becky, Slats Scrapple's girl friend. "Aunt" Abbie was a minor character, an aging spinster. It all took place in the village of Crabtree Corners.

The original Avengers were Thor, Iron Man, The Wasp, The Hulk, and Ant-Man, although The Hulk soon departed the group. The Avengers first appeared in September 1963.

Archie turned 40 in December 1981.

"After you, my dear Alphonse" comes from the early comic strip "Alphonse and Gaston," by F. Opper.

Beetle Bailey and his fellow soldiers are stationed at Camp Swampy. Sergeant Snorkel's first name is Orville.

Dick Tracy became a detective after Jeremiah Trueheart (father of Tess Trueheart, Tracy's fiancée) was shot to death by robbers. The murder occurred in the first week of the strip, which began as "Plainclothes Tracy."

The town of Crystal City, Texas, boasts a statue of Popeye the Sailor, erected by local spinach growers in 1937.

Companies

The world's first supermarkets—stores incorporating both the cash-and-carry and self-service theories of merchandizing—were the Piggly Wiggly stores designed by Clarence Saunders of Memphis, Tennessee. The stores had only one aisle, which began at the entrance and wound back and forth back to the exit. (Saunders supposedly got the idea for the store's name when, riding on a train through Tennessee, he saw a fat pig wiggling its way under a fence.) Once in a Piggly Wiggly store, the customer had to pass every product in order to get out again. Saunders kept developing new ideas for supermarkets. In 1941, he made plans to open a chain of Keedoozle stores, in which each shopper would carry around a kind of pistol-shaped electric key; the foods would be displayed behind glass—like food in an automat—and the customer would stick the key in a slot beneath the product and pull the trigger; the product and size would be printed on a paper tape inside the pistol; the customer would give the tape to the cashier, and the cashier would feed the tape into a machine that would activate a machine in the storeroom, which would begin loading bags . . . The war got in the way of the Keedoozle stores, and Saunders died before he could perfect his Food-electric stores, in which the customers would bag their own groceries and then add up their bill using a special small-sized calculator.

Albert Gerrard noticed that customers wandering through stores sometimes had difficulty locating products, so he arranged all the items in his stores alphabetically and called them Alpha-Beta stores.

It was Michael Cullen who developed the prototype for today's monster grocery stores, and it was the Great

Depression that made such stores so popular—and urgently needed. Cullen's idea was to build a monstrous store in a low-rent district with plenty of parking all around and sell items at a price just above cost. Mr. Cullen renamed himself King Cullen and opened his first store in an abandoned garage on the corner of 171st Street and Jamaica Avenue, in Queens, New York, on August 30, 1930.

The three *M*s in the 3M Company stand for Minnesota Mining and Manufacturing Company.

The *A* and *W* in A&W Root Beer stand for Allen and Wright.

Tiffany's is named for Charles Lewis Tiffany. The elegant store opened September 18, 1837, in lower Manhattan. Sales for the first day totalled $4.98, with a profit the first week of 33¢. During World War I, the Tiffany factory made surgical instruments; during World War II, the factory made precision airplane parts.

Richard Warren Sears began his merchandizing career selling watches. He opened his R. W. Sears Watch Company in 1887, in Minneapolis, but he soon moved to Chicago. In need of a watchmaker to repair his products, he advertised in the Chicago *Daily News* for a watchmaker, and Alvah Curtis Roebuck answered the ad.

When James Cash Penney opened his first store—in 1902 in Kemmerer, Ohio—he called it the Golden Rule.

The Shell Oil Company started out as a novelty shop selling seashells.

L. L. Bean's full name was Leon Leonwood Bean. His brother Guy was able to help him when he started selling through the mail—Guy was the local postmaster.

The name of E. J. Korvette has been the source of great speculation. It was once said to stand for "Eight Jewish Korean Vets." Actually, the E stands for Eugene (Eugene Kerkauf, founder of the store); the J is for Joseph (Joseph Zwillenberg, one of Kerkauf's partners); and Korvette is a misspelling of corvette, the small warship.

The K in K-Mart stands for Kresge, from Sebastian S. Kresge, who founded the store in Detroit, in 1897.

When Herbert and Sidney Hubschman opened a store selling clothes at low prices, one of their competitors complained about "those two bastards from Harrison." The two brothers heard the lament and named their store Two Guys from Harrison; today the store is simply Two Guys.

The Avon Perfume Company got its name because its original owner was fond of Shakespeare: Stratford-on-Avon.

The first store to allow customers to exchange or return merchandise was Wanamaker's in New York.

Burton "Butch" Baskin and Irving Robbins merged their two chains of ice-cream stores in 1948, creating an empire. Irving Robbins takes the ice-cream business seriously—his California home has an ice-cream-cone-shaped swimming pool. At night, the lighted pool is pointed out to airline passengers as a landmark.

When the golden spike was driven at Promontory Point, Utah Territory, uniting the two coasts of the nation with a railroad, George Huntington Hartford renamed his tea store the Great Atlantic and Pacific Tea Company. He did not have stores on the West Coast, but he wanted to cash in on the excitement.

Frank Winfield Woolworth opened the nation's first five-and-dime in Utica, New York, in 1879. The first store failed, but he was successful when he tried again in Lancaster, Pennsylvania. Woolworth had the habit of disguising himself and visiting his stores to shoplift—just to keep his employees on their toes.

Montgomery Ward issued the first mail-order catalog in 1872—it was one sheet of paper. By 1896, the catalog had grown, and Montgomery Ward started to use live models in the illustrations—as a result, the models began receiving proposals for marriage.

Former cab fleet owner John D. Hertz began renting cars in 1923. He called his company The Hertz Drive-Ur-Self System.

Rowland Hussey Macy went to sea and spent four years on a whaling voyage. He then spent two years in San Francisco during the gold rush. Finally, in 1858, he opened the first department store—Macy's.

On April 7, 1818, Henry Sands Brooks opened a clothing store on Catherine and Cherry streets in Manhattan. His two older brothers, Henry and Daniel, joined him, hence Brooks Brothers. The store's trademark is the Golden Fleece, symbol of British woolen merchants.

Cowboys

Famous cowboy actors are usually inseparable from their horses. Following are some well-known cowboy–mount matchups:

Gene Autry:	Champion
Rex Allen:	KoKo
Tom Mix:	Tony
The Cisco Kid:	Diablo
Pancho (Cisco's sidekick):	Lobo
The Durango Kid:	Raider
Roy Rogers:	Trigger
Dale Evans:	Buttermilk
Red Ryder:	Thunder
Little Beaver (Red's sidekick):	Papoose
Hopalong Cassidy:	Topper
The Lone Ranger:	Silver
Tonto (the Ranger's sidekick):	Scout
Tex Ritter:	White Flash

Buffalo Bill Cody appeared in a few films, including *The Life of Buffalo Bill* (1909); *Buffalo Bill's Far West and Pawnee Bill's Far East* (1910); *The Indian Wars* (1913); *Sitting Bull—The Hostile Sioux Indian Chief* (1914); and *Patsy of the Circus* (1915).

William Conrad provided Marshal Matt Dillon's voice in the radio version of "Gunsmoke," a role taken over by James Arness on television.

The Great Train Robbery (1903) was the first film with a plot—the first real movie. This western was filmed in New Jersey, America's film capital until the better weather of Los Angeles, California, lured away the filmmakers.

Chuck Connors, better known as "The Rifleman," played for the Brooklyn Dodgers in 1949 and for the Chicago Cubs in 1951.

The performer who has appeared in the most films was Tom London (1883–1963), born in Louisville, Kentucky. He made his first of 2,000 appearances in *The Great Train Robbery*. He was given the role of the locomotive driver, which happened to be his job in real life. By 1919, he was starring in films under his real name, Leonard Clapham. When he got too old to play lead roles, he became a character actor, usually playing the part of the sheriff in low-budget westerns. His last film was *The Lone Texan* (1959).

John Wayne had a size 18 neck.

In order to facilitate the fast draw so essential to good-guy survival in western movies, a special holster was designed by Arvo Ojala. It is constructed of aluminum with a leather covering. The aluminum doesn't allow guns to stick in the holster, but cowboys must change holsters before riding off—otherwise, the gun would bounce right out.

The name of the powerful steed that bore about Hoss (Dan Blocker) on the television series "Bonanza" was Chub.

William S. Hart, early star of western movies, was so fond of his horse, Fritz, that he gave Fritz screen credit.

Emmett Dalton, youngest of the Dalton brothers—the outlaws who rode with the nefarious Doolin boys—survived all the shootouts and bank robberies to appear in a few motion pictures, including *Beyond the Law*.

Cowboy stars William S. Hart and Tom Mix served as pallbearers at the funeral of Wyatt Earp.

The name of Hopalong Cassidy's ranch was the Bar–20; John Wayne's was called 26 Bar Ranch.

A "ten-gallon" hat holds only three-quarters of a gallon.

During their heyday, cowboys bought most of their gear from general stores or from the Montgomery Ward catalog. Some of the items and their prices:

Winchester rifle: $20.50
Stetson: $10
Colt Peacemaker: $12.20
Holster: $2
Boots: $20
Saddle: $40
Horse: $35
Levi Strauss jeans: $13.50 a dozen

Declaring Independence

When John Hancock signed the Declaration of Independence in large, easy-to-read script, he had a lot to lose—he was one of the richest men in America.

Eight of the men who signed the Declaration were born in the British Isles.

The average age of the signers was 45. Benjamin Franklin was the oldest, at 70; Edward Rutledge was the youngest, at 26.

Of the 56 men who signed the Declaration, 9 died during the Revolution; 5 were captured by the British and tortured before they died; 12 had their homes destroyed by the enemy; 2 lost sons in the army.

In Jefferson's first draft of the Declaration, he included an attack on slavery: he blamed slavery on King George II. Jefferson's text (which was deleted from the final version) read in part: "He [the king] has waged cruel war against human nature itself, violating its most sacred rights of life and liberty in the persons of a distant people who never offended him, captivating and carrying them into slavery in another hemisphere."

The signature of Button Gwinnett is very rare and very valuable; examples have brought as much as $16,000 at auction. Born in England, Gwinnett was a delegate to the Continental Congress from Georgia and a signer of the Declaration of Independence. He died shortly thereafter in a duel, insuring the scarcity and value of anything in his handwriting.

Copies of the Declaration of Independence were sent through the colonies (the original was lost at the printer's shop). In towns throughout the land the document was read to public gatherings. In one South Carolina town, the Declaration was read aloud by a 9-year-old named Andrew Jackson.

The last of the signers to die was Charles Carroll, who died at age 95 in 1832. Carroll—who was the only Catholic to sign the Declaration—was the wealthiest man in the United States when he died. Three years before he died he had been involved in the creation of the first passenger and freight railroad in the United States.

The first public reading of the Declaration of Independence was given by John Nixon on July 8, 1776, in Philadelphia's Independence Square.

There are 16 known copies of the first printing of the Declaration of Independence. Amazingly, one was discovered in 1968 in an out-of-business Pennsylvania bookstore.

During the attack on Fort McHenry—at which time Francis Scott Key wrote the words to "The Star-Spangled Banner"—4 Americans were killed and 24 were wounded.

Demon Weed

John Rolfe is famous for marrying Pocahontas (in 1614). He had already made a name for himself two years earlier by growing the first successful crop of tobacco in the New World.

In August of 1619, the first slaves were brought to the New World. Twenty blacks arrived in Jamestown, Virginia, and were put up for sale. They were bought with tobacco.

Clergymen in colonial Virginia were paid with tobacco rather than gold or silver. Their yearly salary was 16,000 pounds of tobacco.

George Washington raised money for the Continental Army with the slogan "If you can't send money, send tobacco."

It was Oscar Hammerstein, grandfather of the musical-comedy writer, who, in 1883, invented the first practical cigar-rolling machine, making inexpensive cigars possible.

In the colony of Virginia, taxes could be paid in tobacco.

When Samuel Gompers was ordered by his doctor to limit himself to one cigar a day, the labor leader, who had worked as a cigar maker, rolled himself a huge, 12-inch cigar every morning!

Henry Ford was a vehement and vociferous enemy of cigarettes.

Dollars and Dimes

The average U.S. dollar bill has a lifespan of 18 months.

The dollar sign ($) evolved as a bookkeeper's shorthand version of *PS* for "peso"—the symbol helped prevent confusion among all the various international monies in use in the colonies.

The model for the goddess Liberty on the Liberty half-dollar was the wife of poet Wallace Stevens.

A "sawbuck" is a $10 bill. The name comes from the fact that the bills were marked with a capital *X*, the Roman numeral for 10, which resembles the ends of a sawhorse, or sawbuck.

A "C note" is worth $100. The name comes from the Roman numeral *C* for 100. A "G note" is $1,000, short for a "grand," slang for $1,000.

Booker T. Washington was the first black American to appear on a U.S. coin: a 1946, 50¢ commemorative piece. In 1940, his likeness was used on a 10¢ postage stamp.

T he so-called Franklin, or fugio, cent was the first coin issued by the U.S. government. Designed by Benjamin Franklin, the copper penny featured a sundial symbol of Time with the Latin word *Fugio* ("I fly") and, beneath that, a friendly capitalist warning: "Mind Your Business." The dies for the fugio cent were engraved by Abel Buell, a man who had once been imprisoned for counterfeiting.

"Two bits"—the traditional charge for a shave and a haircut—are worth one quarter. The early colonists used a variety of monies from many nations, and of chief importance were the coins of Spain. The Spanish *real*, worth one-eighth of a peso (the famous "piece of eight") was worth 12½¢. Americans called the *real* a "bit," making "two bits" equal to 25¢.

The buffalo-head nickel was designed by James Earle Fraser, famous for his painting *End of the Trail*. The buffalo used as a model was Black Diamond, borrowed from the Bronx Zoo.

There is a great deal of tin mixed into our "copper" pennies; our nickels are made mostly of copper.

The phrase "In God We Trust" first appeared on a bronze 2¢ piece issued April 22, 1864. The Civil War was raging, and many people felt there should be a reference to God on U.S. coins.

Theodore Roosevelt tried to have the inscription "In God We Trust" removed from all U.S. currency.

Frontier dwellers, usually short on cash, used buckskins as currency. From this, the dollar bill came to be known as a buck.

Martha Washington donated some of her silver forks and spoons for the minting of a series of half-dimes, some of the first coins minted by the U.S. government. Martha is the first woman to appear on American paper currency—a $1 bill issued in 1886. She is also the first woman to appear on a U.S. postage stamp—an 8¢ stamp issued in December of 1902.

The first woman pictured on a U.S. coin was suffragette Susan B. Anthony. She and Benjamin Franklin are the only nonpresidents to appear on American coins.

The Latin phrase *E Pluribus Unum* ("One out of many") was suggested as the motto of the United States by Benjamin Franklin, Thomas Jefferson, and John Adams in August of 1776; it first appeared on a U.S. coin in 1786.

The mill (one-tenth of a cent) is the smallest monetary unit in the United States, but the U.S. government doesn't coin mills. The smallest denomination ever minted was the halfpenny, worth 5 mills, made of copper and about the size of today's quarter.

The Indian on the so-called Indian-head penny was not modeled after an Indian. The model was Sarah Longacre, a relative of one of the mint's officials.

The first Continentals—paper money issued by Congress during the Revolution—promised to pay the bearer in Spanish dollars. The Latin motto on the bills gave a disarmingly honest account of current events: *Exitus in dubio est* ("The issue is in doubt").

Gold coins were in short supply during the Civil War, so both sides in the conflict issued paper money. In the North, the banknotes were green—"greenbacks"; in the South, they were blue and gray—"bluebacks" and "graybacks." It was Salmon P. Chase, Lincoln's secretary of the treasury, who chose green as the color for U.S. currency.

The "bluebacks" and "graybacks" issued by the Confederate States of America depreciated badly—by the end of the war, it took 1,200 Confederate "dollars" to make $1.

When Harry S. Truman decided to add a balcony to the second floor of the White House, he changed U.S. currency. The Treasury Department recalled all $20 bills and issued new ones showing the balcony.

Early Americans

Pocahontas's real name was Mataoka. Pocahontas was a family nickname. In England she was known as Rebekah.

To establish friendly relations with Chief Powhatan and his tribes, Captain John Smith brought gifts: a coat and a hat, a greyhound dog, and an English boy named Thomas Savage.

Of the 102 passengers on the *Mayflower*, only 41 were Pilgrims, the religious dissidents. They called themselves Saints and the rest of the passengers Strangers. Miles Standish, John Alden, and Priscilla Mullins were Strangers. The terms came from Paul's Epistle to the Romans: "They confessed that they were saints and strangers on earth."

Henry Wadsworth Longfellow, who wrote *The Courtship of Miles Standish*, was a descendant of two of that poem's main characters—John Alden and Priscilla Mullins. A daughter of Alden and Mullins married the oldest son of Miles Standish.

The Pilgrims aboard the *Mayflower* were influenced to go no farther than Plymouth Rock because their supplies were nearly gone, "especially our beer."

Squanto, friend of the Pilgrims, made a nice living for a while by extracting payments from Indian groups in return for his promise to keep the whites from attacking with their guns.

The idea of planting fish with corn and beans came from the French to Squanto. He, of course, passed it along to the Pilgrims. The proper method to use was three fish to a hole, arranged like spokes of a wheel.

Plymouth Rock was hauled out of place on December 22, 1774, by 30 teams of oxen driven by the Sons of Liberty. Unfortunately, the rock split in two. One half stayed in place and the other half was set on display in the Plymouth Town Square. Many souvenir chips were whittled off the rock until it was removed and fenced in on July 4, 1834. Eventually it became the front step to a warehouse until it was finally rejoined with the other half at its original site in 1880. So the Plymouth Rock we visit today is not quite the same Plymouth Rock stepped on by the Pilgrims (assuming the Pilgrims ever *did* step on it).

Many colonial beds are quite short, not because early Americans were shorter than we are (they were), but because many colonists slept half sitting up, with the head and upper torso supported by feather pillows.

Education

Red schoolhouses were painted red because red was the cheapest paint available.

The original site of the U.S. Air Force Academy was Lowry Air Force Base, Colorado. After three years there, the Academy was moved to Colorado Springs, in 1958.

Original leaders of the Free Speech Movement that began at the University of California in 1964 were Berkeley students Bettina Aptheker, Mario Savio, and Jack Weinberg.

Princeton University was founded in 1746 as the College of New Jersey. It didn't become Princeton until 1896.

Radcliffe College is named for Anne Radcliffe. She was the first woman benefactor of Harvard, in the 1600s.

Colgate University took its name in 1890 from the famous soapmaking family. For 71 years before that, it was Madison University.

New England schoolmasters practiced the democratic but unsettling custom of moving the class to different parts of town during the year in an effort to give each child in the class the opportunity to—at some point in the year—live near school.

Eureka!

Insurance salesman Lewis Edson Waterman was about to close a big deal—the client was ready to sign on the dotted line for an expensive policy. Waterman handed the man his pen, and at that moment the pen spilled ink all over the papers, abruptly ending the business deal. Waterman decided that he'd had enough of leaky pens. He sat down and invented a new way of feeding the ink to the nib, creating the first practical fountain pen in 1884. He made the first pens by hand; he also started a magazine called *Pen Prophet*.

The Band-Aid was first introduced in 1920 by Johnson & Johnson of New Brunswick, New Jersey.

The first canned, strained baby food was made by Daniel F. Gerber in 1929.

When he reached the august age of 83, Ben Franklin noticed that he was getting nearsighted. He carried two pairs of glasses around for a while. When he got tired of fumbling with the glasses, he invented bifocals. For the century after they were first introduced, they were called Franklin spectacles in honor of their inventor.

Eli Whitney didn't make much money from his invention of the cotton gin, but he went on to prosper as a New England gun manufacturer, acquiring lucrative government contracts.

Otis did not invent the elevator. He developed a safety brake for it. (The hydraulic elevator was invented by Britisher William George Armstrong in 1846. A naturalized Britisher, Sir William Siemans, born in Germany, invented the electric elevator in 1880.)

The message "What hath God wrought?" sent by Samuel F. B. Morse as the first telegram, was chosen by Morse's friend Annie G. Ellsworth, whose father was the U.S. patent commissioner. The passage is from Numbers 23:23. That first telegraph message was sent from the Supreme Court chamber in the Capitol building, Washington, D.C.

The first words typed on a practical typewriter were:
C. LATHAM SHOLES, SEPTEMBER 1867.

King Camp Gillette wanted to invent something. He worked for William Painter, inventor of the crown cork—the tin bottle top lined with cork that is flipped off bottles and then discarded. Painter was well aware of his employee's burning desire and one day he said, "Why  don't you invent something that people can use only once and then throw away?" Transformed by the thought, King C. Gillette scrutinized the world, seeking that something that people could use only once and then throw out (making them come back for more, of course). One morning, as he started to shave, he noted that his razor needed sharpening, an onerous task faced by all men with whiskers. It was while he was staring at his dull razor that the idea struck him—disposable blades! He had trouble finding backers for his invention, and it took a long time to develop a method of hardening and sharpening a thin piece of steel to serve as the blade, but Gillette persevered and finally triumphed. In 1901, he patented his razor; in 1903, only 51 razors and

168 blades were sold; in 1904 the number jumped to 90,000. Gillette's original slogan, used during the early 1900s, reflects the change disposable blades introduced throughout the world: "Shave yourself."

Whitcomb L. Judson of Chicago, Illinois, invented the zipper. He got a patent in 1893 for something that he called, with methodical accuracy, the "Clasp Locker or Unlocker for Shoes," a device intended to free humanity from the tedium of contending with shoelaces. This footgear mechanism consisted of two metal chains that could be quickly joined—or unjoined—in a single movement. Judson showed his invention at the Chicago World's Fair in 1893, it attracted attention, and within a few years it had been applied to clothing, giving us the zipper—which has contributed its fair share to the high speed of modern life.

Charles Francis Jenkins invented the conical paper cup (the one that fits into a metal tube dispenser) around 1900.

Clarence "Bob" Birdseye—"the father of frozen food"—got the idea of freezing food while in Labrador. Watching Eskimos freeze fish and caribou meat gave him the idea of freezing food, and he began experimenting with a quick-freezing process. Fish were the usual subjects of his experiments, but he was willing to freeze almost anything (he even tried an alligator once). He patented his process for quick-freezing food in 1923, and his name—with a slight change in spelling—has become a brand name.

Samuel F. B. Morse patented the telegraph in 1832; Morse code was not perfected for another six years. Morse sent his first transatlantic telegram over the Atlantic cable while sitting at his usual table in Delmonico's Restaurant in New York City.

Alexander Graham Bell patented the telephone in 1876. Thomas Alva Edison, fellow American inventor, came up with what he thought was the correct way to answer a phone call—not "Hello," but "Ahoy!"

The first practical cigarette-making machine was patented by James Bonsack of Virginia in 1883.

Ben Franklin was fond of swimming. He invented flippers for both the hands and the feet. The hand flippers are no longer in use; the feet flippers are swim fins.

A man named Cornelius Swartout took out the first patent for a waffle iron, on August 24, 1869.

In 1860, Charles Hill Morgan invented the first commercially feasible automatic machine to manufacture paper bags.

The food blender was invented in 1936 by Fred Waring, a band leader.

Buxom debutante Caresse Crosby (Mary Phelps Jacobs) was tired of cramming herself into a corset. A descendant of Robert Fulton, she was an inventive girl, and one evening in 1914, she got an idea while dressing for a party. Using two handkerchiefs and some ribbon, she fashioned the first bra. Her innovation was an immediate success; she eventually made the mistake of selling her patent to the Warner Brothers Corset Company for a mere $15,000.

The brown paper bag, so essential to supermarkets, was invented by Luther C. Crowell in 1872.

Condensed milk was invented in 1856 by Gail Borden; evaporated milk was invented in 1884 by John B. Meyenberg.

The first practical ballpoint pen was developed in 1945 by Milton B. Reynolds. The pens went on sale at Gimbel's department store in New York City on October 29, 1945. According to business legend, 10,000 were sold on that one day, which is remarkable—the price of the pen was $12.50.

The first hotel in New York City to have an elevator was the Fifth Avenue Hotel, which opened on August 23, 1859. The elevator became a popular tourist attraction; in 1860, the Prince of Wales visited the hotel to have a look.

Charles Burton invented the baby carriage in 1848 in New York City. The hard-to-steer vehicles were not well received on the crowded sidewalks of the city. Collisions with innocent pedestrians were frequent, and the resulting lamentations over the dangerous device were so loud that Burton left the country, went to England, and started constructing his "perambulators" there. He counted among his satisfied customers Queen Victoria, Isabella II of Spain, and the Pasha of Egypt.

The electric fan was invented by Dr. Schuyler Skaats in 1882. Wheeler was awarded a medal for his beneficial tool.

The so-called grocer's claw—a pole with an attached device for grabbing merchandise off high shelves—was invented by Ben Franklin.

Kleenex tissues were first used as gas-mask filters—during World War I.

Neither the Colt .45 nor the Winchester rifle is included in the three inventions that "won the West." The three most important factors in taming the new territory were barbed wire, the portable windmill, and the steel plow.

The first book matches were patented by a lawyer named Joshua Pusey in 1892. Pusey sold the patent to the Diamond Match Company in 1895.

In 1849, Walter Hunt found himself in dire straits. Penniless and in debt for $15, he decided to invent something. He sat down and in just three hours came up with a very useful device—the safety pin. He sold his patent rights for $100 and paid back the debt. Hunt never saw another cent for his invention.

The first home refrigerator was the Domelre, manufactured in Chicago in 1913. The body was made of wood.

Toilet paper was invented by a resident of New York City, a certain Joseph C. Gayetty, in 1857. He called his innovation "Gayetty's Medicated Paper—a perfectly pure article for the toilet and for the prevention of piles." Gayetty's name was watermarked on every sheet.

Thomas Edison's first invention was patented in 1869—the electric voting machine. It wasn't used until the election of 1892.

Benjamin Franklin invented the rocking chair.

Marvin Chester Stone, of Washington, D.C., invented the drinking straw in 1886; he patented it in 1888; the straws were rolled by hand until a machine was developed in 1905.

John Deere invented the steel plow in 1833, making sod-busting a lot easier.

The electric shaver was patented in 1923 by retired army colonel Jacob Schick; the shavers went on sale in 1931.

The first practical typewriter was patented in 1868 by

Christopher Latham Sholes; production of the machines began in 1872. The first typewriters had only capital letters, numbers from 2 to 9, a comma, and a period. They had no back  space, and it was impossible for the typist to see what he or she was typing. The keys were arranged alphabetically (the arrangement of the keys was soon changed and they were put in the order in which they appear in a typesetter's case, still the basic arrangement). One of the first businessmen to see the value in the new machines was Allan Pinkerton, the famed detective.

It was Benjamin Franklin who determined that lightning is composed of electricity. He invented the lightning rod in 1749 and installed the first one, in 1752, on the top of his house in Philadelphia. Franklin did not patent the device; rather, he published directions for making and installing lightning rods in his *Poor Richard's Almanac*, saving the lives of countless people throughout the world. The new invention was quickly adopted everywhere in America except in New England, where God-fearing folk believed that being struck by lightning was the will of God and should not be tampered with.

Henry Ford did not invent the assembly line; Ransom E. Olds (who gave his name to the Oldsmobile) did, and Ford just improved on his basic idea.

Explorers

It is most likely that the first European to set eyes on North America was the Viking Bjarni Herjulfsson. He sailed along the Canadian coast in 986 but did not land. It was in Herjulfsson's boat that Leif Ericsson returned to the New World in 992. (Leif was followed a few years later by his brother Thorvald and, later, the trader Thorfinn Karlsefni.)

What motivated the early explorers of the New World? "We came here to serve God, and also to get rich," was a candid admission from Bernal Diaz del Castillo.

The first permanent settlement of whites in the United States was founded on September 8, 1565, at St. Augustine, Florida. Led by Don Pedro Menéndez de Aviles, the Spaniards destroyed the French settlement at Parris Island, South Carolina, that had been founded in 1562. (Sir Walter Raleigh's first Roanoke colony, which failed, wasn't started until 1587.)

Hernando DeSoto brought 13 pigs to the New World with him. They debarked with the Spanish explorer in 1542 in what is now Tampa, Florida. There may have been wild pigs here before then.

DeSoto's armor protected him completely during his fierce battle with the Choctaws at Mauvilla—except in the posterior, which soon sported an arrow. The explorer finished the fight standing in his stirrups.

Ponce de Leon came to the New World with Columbus in 1493.

Manhattan Island was named Angoulême in 1524 by Giovanni da Verrazano, an Italian explorer piloting a French ship.

Hernando DeSoto was buried in the Mississippi River in 1542.

Explorer Peter Minuit established the fort of New Sweden in 1638 at what is now Wilmington, Delaware. His expedition was sent by Queen Christiana.

The first non-Indian visitor to Arizona arrived in 1539. He was a black slave by the name of Black Stephen, also called Estévan.

The explorer La Salle was killed on the Gulf Coast in 1687 by his band of 20 (reduced from 400 at the expedition's start in 1684). He was left as a meal for the buzzards.

Henry Hudson was set adrift by mutinous crew members in June 1611 in the James Bay section of Hudson Bay. He was never heard of again.

The Grand Canyon was discovered (for the white world) in 1540 by Garcia Lopez de Cardenas, leading an offshoot of the Coronado expedition.

Coronado went in search of the "Seven Cities of Cibola," overflowing with gold and silver, after hearing the tales brought back to Mexico by Fray Marcos de Niza, who had traveled to Arizona in 1539. The person who led Coronado and his soldiers in their search for the Seven Cities was an Indian guide named the Turk by the Spaniards, who told more and more tales of fabulous wealth as the expedition progressed.

The first white person to land on the Pacific Coast of the future United States was Juan Rodriguez Cabrillo in 1542. He landed near San Diego's Ballast Point.

Settlement of the Great Plains was delayed and discouraged by Zebulon Pike's report on his 1805–07 expeditions, in which he described the Plains as "incapable of cultivation" and painted a general picture of desolation. Later, explorer Stephen H. Long of the U.S. Army termed the Nebraska Territory "a great American desert."

Members of the Lewis and Clark expedition learned to relish dog meat, which they bought (live) from Indians along their route. One dog they did not eat was Lewis's Newfoundland, Scannon, who hunted game for the party. Only one person on the expedition died—Sergeant Floyd.

Frederick Albert Cook claimed to have reached the North Pole on April 21, 1908, while Robert E. Peary got there on April 6, 1909. In 1923, Cook was found guilty of mail fraud and sentenced to 14 years in prison. Paroled in 1930, Cook was pardoned just before he died in 1940.

Robert Peary spent 30 hours at the North Pole. With Peary at the Pole were his black assistant Matthew A. Henson and four Eskimos.

The flask of brandy brought to the Pole by Peary in 1909 froze solid although it was carried under his parka. Peary did not mark the Pole with just the U.S. flag. He also planted the insignia of the DAR, the Navy League, the Red Cross, and Delta Kappa Epsilon (his Bowdoin College fraternity).

Fads

The early 1900s saw a great many new dances—the Turkey Trot, the Grizzly Bear, the Kangaroo Dip, and the Bunny Hug. Fifteen women were fired from the staff of the *Ladies' Home Journal* for dancing the Turkey Trot during their lunch hour.

A vaudeville performer named Bill "Bojangles" Robinson holds the record for running backward: he ran 100 yards backward in 13.5 seconds.

Bill Williams of Hondo, Texas, spent a total of 30 days edging a peanut up 22-mile Pikes Peak with his nose. He did it to win a $500 bet.

Alvin "Shipwreck" Kelly invented flagpole sitting. Called "the luckiest fool alive," he began the craze in 1924; by 1929, it had become a national obsession. In 1936, Alvin ate 13 doughnuts while standing on his head on a wooden board sticking out from the roof of a 56-story building in New York City.

The year 1929 witnessed a large number of outrageous contests, such as rocking-chair derbies, talking contests, eating contests, kissing contests, even tree-sitting contests.

The original Frisbees were pie plates from the Frisbee Baking Company of Bridgeport, Connecticut.

One of the longest Monopoly games on record was a 4-man, 264-hour game played in Pinole, California. (The game ended January 5, 1975.)

The Teddy bear was named for President Theodore Roosevelt by its designers, Mr. and Mrs. Morris Michtom, in 1902. It was an immediate success.

The Ouija ("yes") board was invented by brothers William and Isaac Field of Baltimore, Maryland. It was patented in 1892 and became immensely popular during World War I, when it was used to convey messages about the fate of soldiers.

Crossword puzzles became a national fad when Margaret Farrar of the New York *World* (later with the *New York Times* from 1942 to 1974) published the first crossword-puzzle book in 1924.

The chain-letter craze began with Denver's Prosperity Club in April 1935. On Saturday, April 27, 165,000 chain letters were mailed in Denver. The idea swept the country within a few weeks.

The goldfish-swallowing fad was begun on March 3, 1939, by Harvard student Lothrop Withington, Jr., who, on a bet, swallowed a live 3-inch fish at the Harvard Union, in front of assembled reporters.

The first miniature golf course was laid out by Tennessean Garnet Carter in 1927 for his hotel on Lookout Mountain, Chattanooga. By 1930, there were more than 40,000 of the courses all over the country.

A New York architect, Alfred M. Butts, invented Scrabble in 1938. No game manufacturer would accept it, however. Finally, in 1948, a friend, James Brunot of Connecticut, marketed 180 sets. Sales suddenly took off in mid-1952 and reached 1 million by the end of 1953.

Silly Putty was developed by engineer James Wright while working for General Electric. G.E. wasn't interested in the stuff. Ad man Peter Hodgson discovered it in Ruth Fallgatter's toy shop in New Haven, Connecticut, in 1949. Hodgson borrowed $147 to start his business by buying a batch of the stuff and packing blobs of it in plastic-egg containers. It was first marketed in Doubleday bookstores.

The Hula Hoop originated in Australia. It was made of bamboo and used in gym classes. In the United States, it was first produced by the Wham-O Manufacturing Company of San Gabriel, California, in 1957. Made of plastic, it sold for $1.98. It was banned in Indonesia.

The Barbie doll is named after Barbara Handler, daughter of Elliot and Ruth Handler. The senior Handlers developed Barbie and introduced her to the market in 1961. Their company, Mattel, Inc., did quite well. For two years a "Growing Up Skipper" doll was marketed—you turned her arm and her breasts grew.

The skateboard craze was started by out-of-the-water surfers in California in 1961 to keep their skills sharp. By 1964, there were 94 U.S. skateboard manufacturers.

Tom Swifties were all the rage in 1963. They depended on punning use of adverbs. For example: "I'm going on a balloon flight," she said airily.

June Havoc holds the all-time dance marathon record: 3,600 hours, in West Palm Beach, 1934. She was known as Jean Reed. The first marathon fatality was Homer Morehouse of North Tonawanda, New York. In 1923, he danced for 87 hours until his partner gave out. Leaving the dance floor, he collapsed and died.

Heinz Arntz played the piano for 1,054 hours in 1966. He started playing in Düsseldorf, Germany, and ended in Westbury, Long Island.

Pyrography was the *in* thing in 1900. What was it? The craft of burning designs into leather cushions.

Fashions

The miniskirt hit worldwide popularity in 1964. The new Greek military junta outlawed it in 1967. State capitol employees were ordered not to wear the garment by Georgia governor Lester Maddox. Russian designers were allowed to go no farther than two inches above the knee. Who started it all? Either Mary Quant in England or André Courrèges of France.

According to a law established 1619, a person's clothing was taxed in Virginia. This discouraged dandyism.

The Harvard College Year Book of 1649 warned against the fashion then beginning to spread through New England of "wearing long haire after the manner of Ruffians and barbarous Indians."

Two out of every five American women dye their hair.

Forty-four percent of American women over the age of 15 own diamonds. That is the most in the Free World. Italians have the least: only 13%.

In the late 1800s paper patterns for home dressmaking were developed and mass produced by Ellen Demorest. She sold them through her quarterly publication *Mme. Demorest's Mirror of Fashion.*

The dinner jacket made its debut at the Tuxedo Park Country Club ball in Tuxedo Park, New York, worn by Griswold Lorillard, October 10, 1886. It was known after that as a tuxedo.

An early hem-raising fashion was the rainy-day skirt, an innovation of the early 1900s. This skirt was cut off at the ankle to relieve women of the chore of dragging yards and yards of heavy, soaked cloth through rain and snow.

Cold creams weren't available in 1900. Instead, women softened their complexions with a mixture of Vaseline and cucumber.

The ideal of feminine beauty in the early 1900s was, of course, the Gibson Girl, artist Charles Dana Gibson's vision of perfection. She had a counterpart—the Gibson Man, who was perfectly clean shaven. Within a few years of the appearance of the Gibson Man, most American males had shaved their facial hair.

The first president to deliver his inaugural address bareheaded was Theodore Roosevelt, March 4, 1905.

Bras were given cup sizes for the first time in 1939 by Warner Brothers Company of Bridgeport, Connecticut.

Filene's Automatic Bargain Basement lost money for its first 10 years, from 1909 to 1919. Thereafter it ran in the black.

Palm Beach fabric, *the* material for men's summer clothing from the 1930s on, was originally manufactured in Sanford, Maine, by the Goodall Worsted Company, which bought the patent in 1908.

Chanel No.5 got its name because 5 was Coco Chanel's lucky number. (The perfume was introduced in 1922.)

The Du Pont Company introduced the first totally man-made fiber in October 1939, when it offered 4,000 pairs of nylon stockings for sale.

Annette Kellerman, a well-known Australian swimmer, daringly appeared in a one-piece bathing costume sans skirt at Revere Beach, Boston, in 1907. She was arrested for indecent exposure.

The bikini bathing suit was introduced by its creator, Louis Reard, at a fashion show July 5, 1946. It was named after the U.S. atomic bomb test on Bikini Atoll that had occurred four days earlier.

The braless look started in California with designer Rudi Gernreich's topless bathing suits of 1964. It was a popular style—topless dancers were introduced at a San Francisco bar June 19, 1964.

Lacoste shirts are named for René Lacoste, who used the alligator symbol as a member of France's winning Davis Cup tennis team in 1927. (Lacoste had defeated Bill Tilden to win the Cup for his country.) The alligator shirts were first sold in the United States in 1951.

The hip-pocket rivets on Levi's jeans were removed in 1964. They were covered with thread in 1937; the rivets had been scratching school desk chairs.

First and Only

U lysses S. Grant was the first president to change his name. Born Hiram Ulysses Grant, he was mistakenly listed as "Ulysses S. Grant" when he enrolled at West Point. The clerk's error stuck.

James Madison is the only president to actively exercise his authority as Commander-in-Chief of all U.S. military forces. On August 25, 1814, when British troops attacked Washington, D.C., Madison took command of Commodore Joshua Barney's battery a half-mile north of Bladensburg, Maryland, in an attempt to protect the capital.

John Adams (second president) was the only president whose son (John Quincy) was also inaugurated president (sixth).

Franklin Pierce was the darkest horse ever nominated. When his name came up at the Democratic convention of 1832, many people knew who he was, but few could believe their ears. One stunned observer lamented, "Now no one is safe."

Theodore Roosevelt was the first president to ride in an automobile, the first to fly in an airplane, and the first to go underwater in a submarine.

The first Miss America was 16-year-old Margaret Gorman. She was 5'1" tall, weighed 108 pounds, and had measurements of 30-25-32.

Benjamin Franklin established the first fire department in 1736; the first insurance company in 1748; the first circulating library in 1731.

The first person to receive a Social Security check was Mrs. Ida May Fuller of Brattleboro, Vermont. She received the check in 1940 and lived to be over 100, collecting more than $20,000.

The first woman governor in the United States was Mrs. Nellie Taylor Ross. She was elected governor of Wyoming in 1925.

The first native-born American to be sainted was Elizabeth Ann Seton, born in New York on August 28, 1774. She was sainted during the Holy Year of 1975.

The first desegregation sit-in occurred on South Elm Street, Greensboro, North Carolina, at the F. W. Woolworth lunch counter February 1, 1960.

Nathan Bedford Forrest was the Ku Klux Klan's first Grand Dragon in 1867.

Virginia Dare, the first child born of English parents in the New World, was the daughter of Ananias and Eleanor Dare. She was born August 18, 1587.

The first child born of European parents on American soil was Snorro, son of Thorfinn and Gudrid Karlsefni, members of Leif Ericsson's expedition. Snorro was probably born in 1007 in what is now Maine; in later life he served in the government of Iceland.

Benjamin Franklin owned the first bathtub in the colonies.

David Dixon Porter, foster brother of naval hero David G. Farragut, in command of a storeship named *Supply*, landed a shipment of 34 camels at Indianola, Texas, May 14, 1856. The shipment of camels from Smyrna, Turkey, was the first of the species brought to the New World for commercial purposes. The army planned to experiment with them as pack animals.

The first fire engine in America was constructed in 1654 by ironmaker Joseph Jencks.

When the first U.S. census was taken, in 1790, there were 3,929,214 people living in the 13 states.

The first clockmaker to arrive in the United States was William Davis, who landed in Boston in 1683.

The first commercial singles-only weekend was held at Grossinger's in New York's Catskills in 1962. The first singles-only apartment complex was the South Bay Club in Torrance, California, built in 1965.

Calvin Coolidge was the first president born on the Fourth of July (1872, in Plymouth, Vermont).

Harry S. Truman made the first telecast from the White House. He was launching the Food Conservation Program.

In 1958, Ecuador issued a green, 2-sucre postage stamp bearing the likeness of then vice-president Richard M. Nixon, the first stamp with the portrait of an American vice president issued by a foreign country.

Thomas Jefferson was the first president to shake hands. (Washington and Adams had bowed to their callers.)

James Madison was the first president to wear long pants. (His predecessors had all worn knickers.)

Jimmy Carter is the only president to report sighting a U.F.O.

The first bathroom was installed in the New York residence of George Vanderbilt in 1855.

Gerald Ford is the only president to have worked as a male model.

Jimmy Carter is the first president born in a hospital.

John F. Kennedy was the first president born in the twentieth century. (He was born in 1917 and took office in 1961.)

J ohn Quincy Adams was the only president to be a published poet. He wore the same hat for 10 years. (When Chester A. Arthur moved into the White House, he had the entire building cleaned and repaired and got rid of a lot of accumulated paraphernalia—including a pair of Lincoln's pants and a badly worn hat of John Quincy Adams's.)

James Buchanan was the only bachelor president. Other men have served without wives, but Buchanan is the only one who never married.

Alden C. Flagg was one of the holders of the first number—258—in the military draft lottery of 1917. His son, Alden C. Flagg, Jr., was a holder of the first number—158—in the draft lottery of 1940.

The first game marketed by Parker Brothers (in 1885) was Banking, developed by George Swinerton Parker.

In 1835, the U.S. government was debt-free for the first and, thus far, only time in its history.

The first laundromat was called a "washateria." It opened on April 18, 1934, in Fort Worth, Texas, with four machines. Proprietor was J. F. Cantrell.

The first Holiday Inn was built by Kemmons Wilson on U.S. Route 70 in Memphis, Tennessee. It opened in 1952.

First Families

Five children of presidents were born in foreign countries: a son and a daughter of John Quincy Adams—George Washington Adams in Berlin, Germany, and Louisa Catherine Adams in St. Petersburg, Russia; the two sons of Herbert Hoover—Herbert Clark Hoover, Jr., and Allan Henry Hoover were both born in London, England; and a son of Franklin D. Roosevelt—FDR, Jr., was born in Campobello, New Brunswick, Canada.

Four sons of presidents served in presidential cabinets or as subcabinet officials: Robert Todd Lincoln (Garfield's secretary of war); James R. Garfield (Theodore Roosevelt's secretary of the interior); Herbert Hoover, Jr. (Eisenhower's undersecretary of state); Franklin Delano Roosevelt, Jr. (Lyndon Johnson's undersecretary of commerce).

Four sons of presidents were contenders for presidential nominations (but none was chosen): John S. Harrison, son of William Henry Harrison and father of Benjamin Harrison, in 1856; John Van Buren, who preferred to see his father nominated, in 1848; Robert Todd Lincoln, 1884 and 1888; and Robert A. Taft, 1940, 1948, and 1952.

Thomas Jefferson's grandson was the first child born in the White House: James Madison Randolph, January 17, 1806.

George and Martha Washington had no children. Martha had been married before and had four children by that marriage, two of whom survived to adulthood.

Martha Washington was thrifty—she took apart George's worn silk stockings and reknitted them into seat covers.

Mrs. Andrew Johnson taught her husband to read when he was 17 years old.

Lyndon B. Johnson proposed to Lady Bird the day after he met her; they were married two months later.

Edith B. Wilson, Woodrow Wilson's second wife, was a direct descendant of Pocahontas and John Rolfe.

William Henry Harrison and his wife eloped—the only future presidential couple to do so.

Alexander Hamilton was born out of wedlock on the island of Nevis in the British West Indies.

Three of Theodore Roosevelt's four sons were killed serving their country in war: Quentin was killed in World War I; Theodore, Jr., and Kermit died in World War II.

The future Mrs. Calvin Coolidge taught deaf people for three years at the Clarke Institute for the Deaf in Northampton, Massachusetts. Thanks to the experience, she was prepared for life with "Silent" Cal.

John Tyler had the most children of all U.S. presidents: five. He had the help of two wives.

Robert Todd Lincoln arrived at the scene of three presidential assassinations. He joined his father after the shooting at Ford's Theatre; he arrived at the Washington, D.C., railroad station to meet Garfield just after the president had been shot; he arrived at the Pan American Exposition in Buffalo, New York, to meet President McKinley just after *he* had been shot.

Jefferson Davis was the son-in-law of President Zachary Taylor, having eloped with Taylor's daughter Sarah in 1835.

Dolley Madison was addicted to snuff.

Andrew Jackson's wife smoked a corncob pipe.

Zachary Taylor's wife smoked a pipe.

Robert Todd Lincoln, son of Abraham, went to Harvard. Coming home from school on vacation, he fell between two train cars. His life was saved by Edwin Booth, whose brother was soon to kill Robert's father.

Abraham Lincoln's wife, Mary Todd Lincoln, was born in Kentucky. She was accused during the Civil War of being a Southern sympathizer—if not a spy. Four of her brothers—Lincoln's brothers-in-law—wore Confederate uniforms.

First Ladies

The president's wife was first called the First Lady by Mary Clemmer Ames in an article for the *Independent* on March 5, 1877, upon the inauguration of Rutherford B. Hayes.

The term *First Lady* wasn't widely used until a comedy called *The First Lady in the Land,* by Charles Nirdlinger, opened at New York's Gaiety Theater on December 4, 1911. The play was about Dolley Madison.

The president's wife who was youngest when she married was Eliza McCardle Johnson, age 16. The oldest marrying for the first time was Bess Wallace Truman, age 34.

Martha Washington was called Lady Washington while her husband was president.

Dolley Madison was voted a seat in the House of Representatives on January 9, 1844.

Alice Roosevelt, Teddy Roosevelt's daughter, was the White House's number-one nonconformist. She smoked in public (most ladies did not even smoke in private then); she leaped fully clothed into a swimming pool, pulling a congressman along with her; she was a mean hand at poker with the men. She was immensely popular—in the United States and abroad.

Nancy Davis Reagan is not the only (or first) First Lady to have been an actress. Pat Nixon had bit parts in *Becky Sharp* and *Small Town Girl* while she was a college student.

In 1940, Eleanor Roosevelt publicly advocated birth control.

Fish and Shellfish

Goldfish were unknown in the United States until Commodore Matthew Perry opened up Japan to the West in the 1850s. One of the navymen with Perry, Daniel Ammen, brought the first goldfish back from Japan in 1878. The easy-to-care-for fish became popular pets.

Nearly 15% of America's citizens own pet fish.

The largest freshwater fish ever caught in the United States was a 360-pound white sturgeon caught in the Snake River, Idaho, April 24, 1956.

A salmon can swim as far as 3,000 miles to spawn in its home stream—the one in which it hatched four years previously.

Oysters change sex annually throughout life.

The archer fish shoots a spray of water at insects on shore to knock them into the water, where the archer can then gobble them up.

A lobster or a crab can throw a claw—drop the entire leg from its body—at will. It simply grows a new limb as a replacement.

A sea cucumber is an animal that looks like a cucumber—usually; it changes shape while moving around.

Your pet goldfish could live to be 40; most *can* live to 17. Just be sure to keep its water clean and at a steady temperature.

Food Facts

Microwave cooking was discovered accidentally by Percy LeBaron Spencer of the Raytheon Company in the 1940s when microwaves melted a candy bar in his pocket.

Blackstrap molasses, brewer's yeast, yogurt, and wheat germ all became popular in 1950 after being praised in the bestseller *Look Younger, Live Longer*, by Gayelord Hauser. Sales of Kretschmer Wheat Germ doubled that year, and the Dannon Yogurt Company outgrew its plant.

Irish coffee was first served in the United States at the Buena Vista Cafe in San Francisco, California, in 1953. It was an immediate hit.

BHA was approved as a food additive by the FDA in 1954. It had been used commercially since 1947.

In her first television show, Julia Child prepared boeuf bourguignonne.

Weight Watchers was founded by Jean Neditch of Queens, New York, a housewife who lost 71 pounds herself.

The restaurant closed in 1964 by Lester Maddox rather than obey the law and serve blacks was the Pickrick Restaurant in Atlanta.

Colonel Sanders sold his Kentucky Fried Chicken business in 1964 for $2 million plus a lifetime annual salary of $40,000.

Ocean Spray Cranberries introduced cranapple juice in 1965.

Diet Pepsi was offered to the public in 1965 by the Pepsi-Cola Company.

The first freeze-dried coffee was Maxim, introduced by General Foods in 1964. Taster's Choice (Nestlé) appeared on the market in 1966.

The name of the famous bialy (not to be confused with the bagel, which gets its name from a Yiddish word meaning "ring") is named for a burg in Poland—Bialystok.

The carrot followed the Jamestown colonists to America in 1609.

Commercial celery growing in this country was started in the 1870s by Dutch farmers in the Kalamazoo, Michigan, area.

America's first coffee merchant was Dorothy Jones of Boston, who was granted a selling license in 1670.

Baby food labeled "high meat dinner" must contain at least 30% meat; "meat and broth" must contain at least 65% meat; whereas "vegetable and meat" only needs 8% meat.

The blight that killed all edible chestnuts (not horse chestnuts) in the United States occurred in 1904.

Sprigs of elderberry are said to ward off evil spirits.

The generic word for that thick tomato sauce kids love is *catsup*. *Ketchup* is a catsup manufacturer's version of the word.

The boysenberry was developed by Rudolph Boysen. It is

a cross of the blackberry, the red raspberry, and the loganberry. Boysen's few plants were discovered and cultivated during the 1930s by Walter and Cordelia Knott and became the foundation of Knott's Berry Farm.

Mark Twain called cauliflower "cabbage with a college education."

South of San Francisco, on U.S. Route 1, is a 20-foot-high avocado. The avocado originated in Central and South America and was first planted in the United States in Florida in the 1830s. Before 1900, the avocado was called alligator pear, laurel peach, custard apple, and butter pear. Half of a 10-ounce avocado contains 2.4 grams of protein; the avocado is one of the only fruits to contain protein.

Shrimp contains arsenic. Potatoes are laced with solanine. (The average American eats 119 pounds of potatoes per year; if all 119 pounds were eaten at once, the diner would die of solanine poisoning—unless he died of overeating first.)

The pineapple is a berry.

Americans consumed more than 50 billion hamburgers in 1976.

The Bon Vivant food company ended its 108-year history in bankruptcy after Samuel Cochran, Jr., of Bedford Village, New York, supped on Bon Vivant Vichyssoise soup and died of botulism June 30, 1971.

There are no aphrodisiac foods. (If one works for you, it's all in your mind.)

Calling it the "mad apple," nineteenth-century Americans believed the eggplant to be poisonous.

The first U.S. chocolate manufacturing plant started operating in Massachusetts in 1765.

Bagels are not fried, as doughnuts are. They are simmered in water and then baked.

An enormous 1,235-pound brick of cheese was conferred on President Thomas Jefferson; hence the phrase *big cheese*.

Mass production of the candy bar began during World War I, so U.S. soldiers would have a quick pick-me-up.

Coca-Cola was first bottled by Joseph P. Whitehead and Benjamin F. Thomas in Chattanooga, Tennessee. Until then, Coke had been sold only at soda fountains, starting on May 8, 1886, at Jacob's Pharmacy in Atlanta, Georgia, dispensed by Willis E. Venable.

In 1891, New York City's soda fountains outnumbered its saloons.

The shopping cart was developed by Sylvan N. Goldman of Standard Food Markets and Humpty Dumpty Stores. He unveiled his creation on June 4, 1937, in Oklahoma City. Now people could buy much more in a single visit to the grocery store.

The first McDonald's was a Pasadena, California, drive-in opened in 1940 by two brothers, Richard and Maurice McDonald. The drive-in became a self-service restaurant in 1948.

A popular book for Americans faced with food shortages in 1942 was titled *How to Cook a Wolf*, by M.F.K. Fisher.

In 1944, Henry Ford predicted that soybean milk would replace cow's milk by 1949.

As early as 1907, a ban on saccharin was urged by Harvey W. Wiley, a Department of Agriculture chemist.

World War I caused Americans temporarily to rename sauerkraut "liberty cabbage" and permanently to transform German toast into "French toast."

Broccoli was introduced to this country from Italy in 1928 by the D'Arrigo Brothers, California vegetable growers.

People started saying "the greatest thing since sliced bread" after 1930, when the first sliced bread was introduced—it was Wonder Bread.

Where did all those apples come from that were peddled on the streets during the Depression? They were supplied by the International Apple-Shippers' Association. A crate sold for $1.75 and a profit of $1.85 could be made if every apple was sold for 5¢—but often many of the apples were unsaleable.

Pan American Airways served the first airborne hot meals in 1935.

James Beard's first cookbook was *Hors d'Oeuvres and Canapes*, published in 1940.

Baking powder was first available for purchase in the early 1850s.

When Arm & Hammer Baking Soda was introduced to the market in 1867, sales were boosted by the impressive salesman Colonel Powell, who measured in at 7'4".

The ice-cream soda was invented by Robert Green at the Franklin Institute exhibition in Philadelphia, 1874. He ran out of cream to mix with syrup and carbonated water, so he used ice cream instead.

Canned sweet corn was introduced in 1867 by Burnham & Morrill Company of Portland, Maine; canned baked beans followed in 1875. B & M Baked Beans are still being manufactured there.

John Harvey Kellogg was, like many of his fellow Seventh-Day Adventists, a vegetarian. "How can you eat anything that looks out of eyes?" he asked.

Apple seeds were brought to America by both the Jamestown colonists and the *Mayflower* Pilgrims. Johnny Appleseed (John Chapman) died in 1845 in Fort Wayne, Indiana. More than 75 million bushels of apples are stored over the winter in the United States. The total crop is 200 million bushels.

Green apples do not give you a stomachache. Eating them quickly and not chewing them thoroughly—because they're bitter—is what gives you the ache.

Peter Cooper invented sweetened, flavored gelatin—the forerunner of Jell-O—in the 1840s. It wasn't popular. In the 1890s, Charles Knox revived the idea and packaged plain powdered gelatin. This did catch on.

"Natural" breakfast cereals were introduced by the major food companies in 1972:
Heartland Natural Cereal (Post)
Country Morning (Kellogg)
Quaker 100% Natural (Quaker Oats)
Granola (General Mills).

Imitation milk was marketed in Arizona in 1967. Brands included Moo, Farmer's Daughter, and Country Cousin.

Remember chlorophyll? At its height of popularity in 1952

and 1953, sales of chlorophyll products hit $120 million. (By 1955, the figure was a mere $10 million.) You could even choose from among eight brands of chlorophyll-flavored dog food. Dr. Benjamin Grushkin was the man who developed the method of making chlorophyll water soluble.

The cabbage made its appearance in North America when it was planted in Canada in 1541 by Jacques Cartier.

The first line of Martha Washington's favorite recipe is "Take fifty eggs . . ."

Liederkranz cheese is named for the choral society its inventor, Emile Frey, belonged to. The cheese was introduced in 1892.

Flaked breakfast cereal was developed by John Harvey Kellogg. He and his brother Will Keith Kellogg marketed it as Granose, beginning in 1895.

Cracker Jack made its debut in 1896, but prizes weren't included in the boxes until 1912.

The earliest hamburger stand was Louis's Lunch in New Haven, Connecticut, a three-seater. In 1900, proprietor Louis Lassen's menu included hamburger patties sandwiched between toast.

In the early 1900s, *the* way to eat was called "fletcherizing." It meant chewing each bite of food 30 times, minimum. Fletcherizing was advocated by nutritionist Horace Fletcher.

Almonds were first transported to the United States —California—by priests from Spain.

It isn't necessary to buy expensive insect repellent. Simply apply garlic instead. How can you rid your breath of garlic? Chew a sprig of fresh parsley.

Biscuits became crackers in 1801, when Josiah Bent's bakery opened in Milton, Massachusetts, and produced a multi-rolled, crisp water biscuit that cracked when bitten into.

One of the first items exported from the American colonies was cranberries.

Spaghetti was introduced to the United States in 1787 by Thomas Jefferson.

Fortune cookies are purely American, developed for U.S. Chinese restaurants. (Brooklyn may be where it all started.)

Golf

Jack Nicklaus won the U.S. Open (in a playoff against Arnold Palmer) in his first year as a pro, 1962.

Gary Player won $26,000 as the winner of the U.S. Open in 1965; he gave it all to his caddy and to charity.

The first public golf course was in New York City—it opened in Van Cortlandt Park.

In 1912, a contestant entered the qualifying round of the Shawnee Invitational for Ladies at Shawnee-on-Delaware, Pennsylvania. She hit her tee shot on the sixteenth hole into a river, where the ball floated. She hit at the ball from a rowboat. Her score for the hole is the worst ever recorded: 160 strokes.

Roberto DeVincenzo lost the 1968 Masters Tournament when he turned in a scorecard that wasn't right. Second-place Bob Goalby was named the winner.

Siwanoy Country Club in Bronxville, New York, was the site of the first professional golf tournament April 10, 1916.

Habits of the First Office

For his inauguration as president in 1904, Teddy Roosevelt had the Apache chief Geronimo released from a military prison in Indian Territory, where he was being held, long enough to ride in an open car up Pennsylvania Avenue. For the occasion, Geronimo wore a fancy black silk top hat.

Calvin Coolidge didn't let his wife supervise any of the details of their life in the White House. Coolidge did it all; even the menus and housekeeping plans were submitted to him for approval.

After moving into the White House, Calvin Coolidge put a rocking chair out on the front porch. He sat in it evenings, smoking cigars.

Calvin Coolidge always wore gloves while fishing. He held the rod; Secret Service men had to attach the squiggling bait to the hook.

Even at age 57, John Quincy Adams was fond of flinging off his clothes and jumping naked into the Potomac for an invigorating swim.

Richard Nixon's favorite president was Woodrow Wilson. He had a picture of Wilson hung on the wall of his office and had Wilson's desk moved into the Oval Office. He liked to put his feet up on it.

The first telephone in the White House was installed for Grover Cleveland in the late 1880s. When the White House phone rang, Cleveland answered it himself.

From 1860 to 1897—from Lincoln to Cleveland—all U.S. presidents wore beards.

All presidents have to shake a lot of hands. McKinley was renowned for his prowess at handshaking—an endless field of extended hands did nothing to dampen his spirit or slow his famous pumping arm. (He was assassinated while shaking hands.) Richard M. Nixon took to wearing a special glove with steel ribbing to make handshaking easier and less chafing.

John Quincy Adams went to bed promptly at 11 p.m. and awakened every morning at 5.

William Howard Taft frequently fell asleep after dinner, during conferences, and at public ceremonies.

Calvin Coolidge slept 11 hours each day. He went to bed at 10 p.m. and got up between 7 a.m. and 9 a.m.; in the afternoon, he napped anywhere from 2 to 4 hours.

Gerald Ford sleeps only four hours each night.

Ulysses S. Grant, Theodore Roosevelt, and Woodrow Wilson were all wearing Brooks Brothers suits when they took their oaths of office.

Abraham Lincoln was the first president to wear a beard.

Holidays

Thanksgiving Day was celebrated only in New England until Abraham Lincoln made it a national holiday in 1863.

Each state determines what holidays will be observed within its boundaries. The president and Congress can declare legal holidays only for the District of Columbia and federal employees.

The only holidays officially observed in all 50 states and the District of Columbia are: New Year's Day, the Fourth of July, Labor Day, Veterans' Day, Thanksgiving Day, and Christmas Day.

Flashlight Safety Day is observed annually on the shortest day of the year. August is Sandwich Month.

It is considered bad luck to hang your new calendar before sunrise on New Year's Day. If your first visitor on New Year's Day is a woman, you will have bad luck that year, but your luck will be good if the visitor is a man.

The Emancipation Proclamation was issued January 1, 1863.

It has been calculated that the groundhog makes a correct weather prediction only 28% of the time when he (or she) emerges on February 2, Groundhog Day.

Theodore Roosevelt's wife and mother both died on the same day—Valentine's Day, February 14, 1884.

Illinois was the first state to make Lincoln's birthday a legal holiday, in 1892.

George Washington's birthday was celebrated while Washington was still alive. The first public celebration was in Richmond, Virginia, held on February 11, 1782, which was the birthday under the Julian calendar. The first public celebration on February 22 was held in New York City, 1783.

The women of Liberal, Kansas, hold a pancake race every Mardi Gras, or Shrove Tuesday. The winner must cross the finish line first after having successfully flipped her pancake three times during the race on the griddle she is carrying. The race is patterned after a similar one in Olney, England.

Easter lily bulbs were brought to this country from Bermuda by Mrs. Thomas P. Sargent in the 1880s. They were then grown by Philadelphia nurseryman William Harris.

President Lincoln was shot on Good Friday (April 14), 1865.

Good Friday is the best day to wean a baby. If you break pottery on this day, you will have good luck. And it's the day you should plant potatoes.

According to superstition, wearing three new things on Easter Sunday will bring you luck for the coming year; prosperity will be yours if your Easter egg has two yolks; a white Christmas will result in a green Easter (while a green Christmas brings a white Easter).

Arbor Day was begun by J. Sterling Morton, an 1854 settler in Nebraska. On the first Arbor Day, observed April 10, 1872, in Nebraska, over 1 million trees were planted.

Mother's Day was originated by Anna M. Jarvis (never a mother herself) of Philadelphia, who arranged a special church service in memory of her mother, Mrs. Anna Reese Jarvis, who had died on May 9, 1905. Services were held in Grafton, West Virginia, and in Philadelphia. The West

Virginia services were conducted by Dr. H. C. Howard. Mother's Day was officially recognized in 1914.

An official Father's Day was initiated by Mrs. John Bruce Dodd of Spokane, Washington, in 1910, to honor her father, William Jackson Smart. Mother-in-Law Day was started by Gene Howe of Amarillo, Texas, March 4, 1934, to honor his mother-in-law, Mrs. W. F. Donald.

Memorial Day originated in the town of Waterloo, New York, the brainchild of druggist Henry C. Welles, to honor Civil War dead. The first observance was May 5, 1866, with speeches by Union general John B. Murray and the Reverend Dr. Samuel Gridley. (Other towns, however, also honored the war dead soon after the war's end.)

The Fourth of July was first celebrated in Philadelphia just one year after the Declaration of Independence was adopted by the Continental Congress. (The only signer of the Declaration on July 4, 1776, was John Hancock; others didn't begin signing until August 2.)

Christmas was not a legal holiday in the United States until 1890; the first state to legalize it was Alabama, in 1836—it was not a legal holiday in New England until 1856.

Labor Day was begun September 5, 1882, by the Central Labor Union of New York City at the suggestion of Peter J. McGuire, a leader of the Knights of Labor and the United Brotherhood of Carpenters and Joiners.

December 7, 1865, was officially designated as Thanksgiving Day by President Andrew Johnson. He had forgotten to proclaim the last Thursday in November as turkey day that year.

The first U.S. Thanksgiving Day was observed on December 4, 1619, at Berkeley Plantation, Virginia. It was also observed by the 30 Berkeley settlers aboard their ship, *Margaret*, November 30.

From 1659 until 1681, it was illegal to observe Christmas Day in the Massachusetts colony. Anyone caught celebrating the day—by feasting or failing to work—was subject to a 5-shilling fine.

The first American Christmas cards were produced by Louis Prang, a German immigrant, in Boston around 1875. His cards were enormously popular until 1890, when cheap European imports flooded the market. Prang stopped making cards rather than compromise on quality.

How Odd!

Norman Mattoon Thomas, socialist leader, ran for president six times—a record thus far—in 1928, 1932, 1936, 1940, 1944, 1948. He got his highest vote in 1932, during the Depression: 800,000.

Theodore Roosevelt shocked the nation—and the world—when he invited Booker T. Washington to dinner at the White House. When the shocking news reached distant Hong Kong, a Britain was moved to exclaim, "I hear your president believes in breaking down all the barriers between the races."

James Garfield made some of his campaign speeches in German.

Although Franklin Roosevelt gave only 27 fireside chats in 6 years, the importance of them was so great that Americans remember them as weekly broadcasts.

Lyndon B. Johnson upset many bashful Americans by swimming nude in the White House swimming pool. (The White House pool was built under the supervision of Ulysses S. Grant, III, Director of Public Buildings. Franklin D. Roosevelt was the first president to use it. It is located at the site where Thomas Jefferson had his chicken coops.)

No president of the United States was an only child.

Thomas Jefferson and John Adams died the same day: July 4, 1826, exactly 50 years after signing the Declaration of Independence. As their deaths approached, the two men—each very much aware that the other was near death—wanted to be the last to go. As Adams died, he murmured, "Thomas Jefferson still survives." He was wrong. Jefferson had died a few hours earlier, his last words being, "Is it the fourth?"

Before taking the office of president, Grover Cleveland served as a sheriff—without the aid of an executioner. The future president hanged criminals himself.

Important Meals

During the presidential administration of Rutherford B. Hayes, no alcohol was served in the White House. Hayes's wife (nicknamed "Lemonade Lucy") forbade alcohol—along with tobacco and dancing. Guests at presidential meals managed to survive by means of various subterfuges, including oranges filled with special frozen punch—the primary ingredient was rum.

Andrew Jackson's favorite breakfast was turkey hash on waffles.

Stonewall Jackson refused to eat pepper.

Thomas Jefferson was quite a gourmet, and he introduced many foreign foods at his dinners at Monticello, including macaroni, anchovies, olive oil, and Parmesan cheese.

Harry S. Truman's favorite drink was buttermilk laced with a good dose of bourbon.

When Lyndon Johnson gave barbecues at his ranch in Texas, he served his guests steaks cut into the shape of the state of Texas.

Abraham Lincoln never had more than a cup of coffee for breakfast.

When Ronald Reagan gave up smoking, he started eating jelly beans. His favorite brand is Jelly Belly's. (When actor Telly Savalas gave up smoking, he took to sucking Tootsie Roll pops.)

Will Rogers's favorite food was chili con carne; he called it "the bowl of blessedness."

Mark Twain ate a thick steak with mushroom gravy for breakfast every morning.

Teddy Roosevelt's favorite food was rare steak.

President Wilson drank a glass of grapefruit juice and ate two raw eggs every morning for breakfast. His favorite lunch was chicken salad.

George Washington was very fond of barbecues.

The first person to eat fresh—not dehydrated—food in outer space was John Young, who took part in the first multimanned flight with Gus Grisson beginning on March 23, 1965. Young took with him a corned-beef sandwich, which he took out and ate during the flight. He got in trouble with NASA authorities when the floating crumbs began to clog up the computers.

Medicine

The birth-defect-causing drug thalidomide was barred from the market by FDA employee Frances Kelsey, a medical doctor and pharmacologist. President Kennedy awarded Dr. Kelsey a distinguished public service medal on August 17, 1962.

Laetrile was patented in 1950 by Ernst T. Krebs.

Jonas Salk shared the 1954 Nobel Prize for developing polio vaccine with three other bacteriologists: John F. Enders, Frederick C. Robbins, and Thomas H. Weller.

Dramamine was developed as an antiallergy drug. It was discovered to help motion sickness when a patient took the drug before riding on a streetcar.

Bayer Aspirin was acquired by Sterling Drug Company in 1919 from the United States government, which had seized the U.S. Bayer Company as spoils of war from its German parent company.

When George Washington became the first president of the United States, in 1789, the life expectancy at birth for Americans was 34 years for men and 36 years for women.

Before the arrival of Columbus, there was no type-B blood in the Americas; American Indians were all either type A or type O.

The average married woman in seventeenth-century America gave birth to 13 children. (Benjamin Franklin, born in 1706, was the fifteenth child born to a Boston soapmaker.)

John Greenwood thrilled no one when he invented the dental drill in 1790. Greenwood had already made a name for himself in dental history when he made a nice pair of false teeth for George Washington using elephant and hippo tusks.

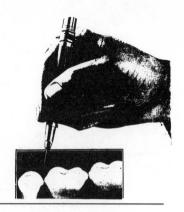

The average American spends about $600 a year on medical expenses.

Colonial remedies were sometimes rather unpalatable. One treatment for diphtheria was to soak cow stool and gargle the resulting liquid. Another use for cow manure was as a cure for toothache—fresh manure was to be pressed on the cheek. Chicken pox sufferers were advised to stretch out on the floor of the chicken coop until a black hen passed over. (It might have been a long wait if your flock didn't include a black hen.)

Lydia E. Pinkham's Vegetable Compound (21% alcohol) was enthusiastically promoted by leaders of the Women's Christian Temperance Union. If Lydia Pinkham's wasn't strong enough for you, you could always try Hostetter's Stomach Bitters, good for whatever ailed you at 44% alcohol.

The application of leeches—to suck out all that bad blood—was unfortunately very popular with doctors until the nineteenth century. It was such common medical practice that doctors were called leeches. George Washington is one of the many early Americans whose death can be attributed to "bleeding" by leeches.

Dr. Samuel A. Mudd, in accordance with the Hippocratic Oath, set the broken leg of John Wilkes Booth, after Booth had assassinated Lincoln. It was a mistake. A Southern sympathizer, Mudd was sentenced to life imprisonment. He remained true to his profession and became a hero when, in 1868, he put an end to a yellow fever epidemic raging in the prison. President Johnson pardoned him in 1869.

The first medical director of the American Red Cross was Charles Richard Drew, a pioneer in blood plasma research. He resigned his post when the U.S. armed forces made it a rule that all blood donations be labeled and segregated by race. Drew was black—his blood would have either been refused or would have been used to treat only black servicemen.

Most American women outlive their husbands by 7.6 years. That's the most in the western world. The least is in Ireland, where 4.9 years divide the death of spouses.

One out of every four Americans suffers back problems.

One out of every six American doctors is a woman; in the Soviet Union, four out of five doctors are women.

Memorable Remarks

The last words Abraham Lincoln heard were part of the play he was watching, *Our American Cousin*. An actor named Harry Hawk (in the role of Asa, "the American cousin"), alone on the stage, said, "Don't know the manners of good society, eh? Well, I guess I know enough to turn you inside out, old gal—you sockdologizing old man-trap." It was at that instant, as the audience began to laugh, that John Wilkes Booth pulled the trigger.

John Wilkes Booth's last words were, "Tell mother I died for my country. I have done what I thought was for the best."

Phineas T. Barnum, the great circus promoter, never said, "There is a sucker born every minute." He did, however, say, "The American public likes to humbugged."

Eight-year-old Virginia O'Hanlon was worried. Francis P. Church allayed her fears in an editorial in the New York *Sun* in December of 1897, writing, "Yes, Virginia, there is a Santa Claus."

George Washington's Farewell Address wasn't a presidential speech. Instead, it was published in Philadelphia on September 19, 1796.

Horace Greeley publicly and repeatedly denied ever having said "Go west, young man." It was John Lane Soule who coined the famous phrase, using it in an article in the *Express* of Terre Haute, Indiana, in 1851. In an effort to give Soule proper credit for the phrase, Greeley reprinted the *Express* article in his New York *Tribune*. No one paid any attention—Greeley is still credited with the statement.

Robert E. Lee, commander of the Confederate troops during the Civil War, is remembered for having said, "It is well that war is so terrible—we should grow too fond of it." He made the remark on December 13, 1862, at the bloody battle of Fredericksburg. He was watching Confederate soldiers weep—they were upset because they had been ordered *not* to charge into Union artillery fire.

General William Tecumseh Sherman claimed he could not recall ever saying "War is hell." He did own up to saying "War at best is barbarism," and in a speech to war veterans in 1880, he said, "There is many a boy here today who looks on war as all glory, but, boys, it is all hell."

Henry ("Light Horse Harry") Lee, brilliant cavalry commander during the American Revolution, was the author of the famous description of George Washington: "A citizen, first in war, first in peace, and first in the hearts of his countrymen." Henry Lee's son earned fame in another American war: Robert E. Lee.

The proud taunt "Tell it to the marines!" was first used in a novel by Sir Walter Scott, where it appears in a form less flattering to the tough leathernecks: "Tell that to the marines—the sailors won't believe it."

Daniel Boone, intrepid frontiersman and blazer of the Wilderness Trail, was once asked if he had ever been lost. "No," replied Boone, "I can't say as ever I was lost, but I was once bewildered for three days."

In October of 1797, French foreign minister Talleyrand tried to bribe the American government—he demanded the tidy sum of $250,000 to call off French attacks on American shipping. Charles C. Pickney, American ambassador to France, is famous for having responded, "Millions for defense, but not a cent for tribute." He never said it. What he said was "Not a penny, not a penny." (The more memorable remark was spoken by Robert G. Harper at a dinner in honor of John Marshall.)

Wealth has never been essential to success in American politics. The great Daniel Webster—the famous statesman whose speech in the Senate on January 26, 1830, included the immortal phrase "Liberty and Union, now and forever, one and inseparable!"—was once sued for failure to pay a butcher bill.

Gail Borden invented condensed milk in 1856. Twenty years earlier, in March of 1836, he had earned fame of another sort when he created a famous American rallying cry. As a newspaper publisher, he had printed the Declaration of Independence for the State of Texas beginning with the headline "Remember the Alamo!"

Chicago mayor Richard Daley really did say, "The policeman isn't there to create disorder, the policeman is there to preserve disorder" and "Together we must rise to ever higher and higher platitudes."

Phineas T. Barnum's last words were, "How were the circus receipts today at Madison Square Garden?"

O. Henry's last words were "Turn up the lights. I don't want to go home in the dark."

Men and Monuments

Before Uncle Sam came along, Americans saw themselves in Brother Jonathan, a character who became a synonym for America during the Revolution. Britains and their Tory allies called Americans "Jonathans" (after "Jonathan the Yankee," a term of mild contempt). George Washington made the name popular. He had a secretary named Jonathan Trumball and was fond of saying, "We must consult Brother Jonathan." Brother Jonathan made his stage debut in 1787 as the comic Yankee in Royall Tyler's *The Contrast*, the first comedy written by an American. Like "Yankee Doodle," Brother Jonathan was originally a figure of contempt—like the song, he was happily embraced by the American revolutionaries and became a symbol of their spirit.

Samuel Wilson, a meat packer in Troy, New York, supplied meat to the U.S. Army during the War of 1812. Wilson was known to his friends as "Uncle Sam." The crates containing his rations were stamped "U.S." (for United States), and his workers joked that the letters stood for "Uncle Sam." Their joke spread, and Uncle Sam became a familiar cartoon character, a symbol of the nation in the same way that John Bull is the symbol of Britain. Congress made it official in 1961, recognizing Uncle Sam as our national symbol.

The actual name of the Statue of Liberty is Liberty Enlightening the World. The words inscribed on the base of the statue are from the sonnet "The New Colossus," by Emma Lazarus.

Frédéric Auguste Bartholdi, sculptor of the Statue of Liberty, used his mother as the model for Liberty.

The iron framework of the Statue of Liberty was designed by Gustav Eiffel, who is famous for a later accomplishment, the Eiffel Tower.

The Statue of Liberty is 46 feet higher than the Colossus of Rhodes, one of the seven wonders of the ancient world.

The first college fraternity was Phi Beta Kappa, founded in 1776 at William and Mary College in Williamsburg, Virginia. The first sorority was Alpha Delta Pi, formed by 16 women at Wesleyan College in Macon, Georgia, on May 15, 1851. Named the Adelphian Society, that name was changed to Alpha Delta Phi in 1904; in 1913 to Alpha Delta Pi.

George Washington's home, Mount Vernon, was treated as neutral territory by both sides during the Civil War.

Among the decorations at Mount Vernon was the key to the Bastille. Lafayette sent it to Washington after its fall in 1789.

The Pentagon is the world's largest office building; it is equipped with 25,000 telephones.

The Capitol building has 540 rooms.

The Washington Monument—the tallest all-masonry structure in the world—sinks an average of 6 inches every year.

Robert Mills, designer of the Washington Monument, was the first native-born professional architect in the United States.

The word *Pennsylvania* is misspelled in the inscription on the Liberty Bell.

The White House had a telephone before it had indoor plumbing.

The White House has 132 rooms.

The largest museum in the world is the American Museum of Natural History in New York, founded in 1874. It is composed of 19 connected buildings covering 23 acres of floor space.

The oldest house in America is in Santa Fe, New Mexico, and was constructed entirely of mud.

The Metropolitan Opera House in New York City is the largest opera house in the world, with a seating capacity of 3,800. The stage is 243 feet wide and 146 feet deep.

Mike Fink, legendary keelboatman on the mighty Mississippi, was probably born sometime around 1770 and may have died in 1823. It's hard to say, for there are over 11 extant versions of his death.

The Liberty Bell in Independence Hall, Philadelphia, was first cast in London in 1752; it was recast in Philadelphia in 1753; it cracked on July 6, 1835, tolling, with muffled clapper, for the funeral parade of U.S. Chief Justice John Marshall.

Benjamin Franklin didn't like the selection of the eagle as our national symbol. He called it a bird of bad moral character. Franklin suggested using the turkey instead.

Money Makes the World Go Around

Wiliam McKinley is pictured on the $500 bill, Grover Cleveland on the $1,000, James Madison on the $5,000, Salmon P. Chase on the $10,000, and Woodrow Wilson on the $100,000. Thomas Jefferson is pictured on the $2 bill. The $2 bill issued until 1966 showed Monticello on the reverse side. The $2 bills issued after April 13, 1976, show the signing of the Declaration of Independence.

The Lincoln Memorial was added to the penny in 1958, 50 years after Lincoln's head was put on the coin.

Andrew Carnegie donated more than $350 million to charity during his lifetime.

Not to be outdone by Carnegie, John D. Rockefeller seeded the Rockefeller Foundation with $100 million on May 14, 1913.

Turn-of-the-century multimillionaire Russell Sage saved money by never buying (or wearing) underwear.

More About Eve

More males are conceived and born than females: 120 males conceived for every 100 females, and 105 males born for every 100 females.

Girl babies start out and keep on smiling oftener than boy babies.

The death rate at any age is higher for men than for women. This even holds true for fetuses.

Men's bodies metabolize food more quickly than women's bodies. That's why men can take in more calories and not gain weight.

The Declaration of Independence was printed by Mary Katherine Goddard.

Those Virginia Slims ads aren't completely untrue. In New York City in 1904, a young woman was jailed for smoking a cigarette publicly. She was caught puffing away while taking a drive in an open car.

Major household chores used to be assigned to particular days of the week: Monday—laundry; Tuesday —ironing; Wednesday—sewing and baking; Thursday—upstairs cleaning; Friday—downstairs cleaning; Saturday—more baking; Sunday—cooking Sunday dinner.

The first witch officially executed in Massachusetts, home of the famous Salem witch trials, was Achsah Young. She met the hangman on May 27, 1647.

The Mormon practice of polygamy began when founder Joseph Smith announced, in July 1843, a revelation from God that virgins could not enter heaven. Smith's wife Emma took a dim view of the revelation.

Amelia Earhart's husband was named George Putnam.

Betsy Ross was married five times. Her first husband was the one named Ross.

The steamship *Baltic* arrived in New York harbor on September 27, 1907, with an unusual cargo—1,002 unmarried women, seeking husbands in the United States.

Mother's Tongue

There are four states in the United States in which more than 10% of the population uses French as their mother tongue: Louisiana, New Hampshire, Maine, and Rhode Island. In Louisiana, 15.8% speak French.

English has the largest vocabulary of all the world's languages.

By the year 1643, even though it was ostensibly ruled by the Dutch, New Amsterdam (New York) had an international flavor, with 20 different nationalities speaking 18 different languages.

According to the U.S. census of 1970, English was the mother language of only 82.1% of native-born Americans.

Alabama has the highest percentage of native-born citizens for whom English is the mother language: 94.3%.

Rhode Island has the highest percentage of native-born speakers for whom Italian is the mother language: 7.1%.

In North Dakota, 14.4% of the native-born speakers speak German as their mother tongue; in New Mexico, the language is Spanish, and 31.9% of the people born in that state speak it.

The Navajo language was used with great success as a code by the United States during World War II.

Movies

In Mickey Rooney's Andy Hardy series, Lewis Stone plays the father, Judge Hardy, Fay Holden is Mrs. Hardy, and Cecilia Parker is Andy's sister, Marian. The first Judge Hardy was Lionel Barrymore. The last Andy Hardy movie was *Love Laughs at Andy Hardy*, made in 1946.

In *My Little Chickadee*, W. C. Fields plays Cuthbert J. Twillie, a snake-oil salesman, and Mae West is Flower Belle Lee, a social outcast.

D. W. Griffith's cameraman was Billy Bitzer.

Johnny Weissmuller's ringing Tarzan-of-the-Apes call was a combination of five sounds, including his own unadorned scream, high C hit by a soprano, and a hyena's howl, recorded and then played backward.

Marni Nixon was the singing voice for Margaret O'Brien in *Big City* (1948), Deborah Kerr in *The King and I* (1956), Natalie Wood in *West Side Story* (1961), and Audrey Hepburn in *My Fair Lady* (1964). (She has appeared on screen only once: a bit part in *The Sound of Music*.)

In the movie *Million Dollar Mermaid*, Esther Williams played real-life Australian-born swimmer Annette Kellerman.

The demon in *The Exorcist* was voiced by Mercedes McCambridge.

Hedy Lamarr and composer George Antheil received a patent in 1942 for a secret torpedo-communications device.

The little statue designed by George Stanley in 1928 for award by the Academy of Motion Picture Arts and Sciences was given its popular name by Academy librarian Margaret Herrick, who remarked that it looked just like her uncle Oscar.

The woman who represents the Statue of Liberty in all Columbia Pictures openers is Jane Chester.

Thomas Edison used his 1899 film patents to organize the Motion Picture Patents Company and establish a monopoly over movie making. To escape the New York–based monopoly, independents moved to Los Angeles. Sabotage and physical assault were the norm all during the early days of the film business. Cecil B. deMille toted a loaded six-gun with him while filming his first movie, *The Squaw Man*, in 1913.

Marian Crane (played by Janet Leigh) is stabbed in the shower in *Psycho*—in the Bates Motel.

The film *Dog Day Afternoon* was based on a real incident: John Wojtowicz robbed a bank in 1972 to get money for a sex-change operation for his boyfriend, Ernest Aron. The heist was not a success, but the movie was—Wojtowicz was able to finance the operation with his income from the film.

The creator of Hopalong Cassidy was Clarence E. Mulford, a marriage-license clerk who lived in Brooklyn, New York, and had never been out west. How did Hoppy get his name? Shot in the knee by a rustler, he declared he could "hop along with the rest" of the posse. Hoppy first appeared in print in *Outing* magazine in 1907. Mulford was paid $90 for the story.

The African Queen was originally intended to star David Niven and Bette Davis.

The six Thin Man films starring William Powell and Myrna Loy were *The Thin Man* (1934), *After the Thin Man* (1936), *Another Thin Man* (1939), *Shadow of the Thin Man* (1941), *The Thin Man Goes Home* (1944), and *Song of the Thin Man* (1947).

A *gidget* (says the movie) is a girl who is about 5'2" tall—small, but not a midget.

There was no president of the Motion Picture Association from 1963, when Eric Johnston died, until April 25, 1966, when Jack Valenti was elected to the position.

No less than 40 Blondie movies were made. Sixty-five Hopalong Cassidy epics were filmed between 1935 and 1948.

Mr. Blandings Builds His Dream House was based on an account published in 1946 by Eric Hodgins telling of his losing financial battle to restore an old farmhouse. Hodgins spent $56,000 fixing up a house on Long Mountain Road in New Milford, Connecticut, and sold it in 1945 for $38,000.

The film *Citizen Kane*, a thinly disguised study of William Randolph Hearst, was ignored by Hearst newspapers. They neither reviewed nor advertised the film.

One of Raquel Welch's four lines (the most comprehensible) in *One Million Years B.C.* was, "Ur-Loana-gunkl-Tumak."

Fidel Castro worked as an extra in Hollywood and appeared in a few films, including *Bathing Beauty* (1944), starring Esther Williams.

The Perils of Pauline (1914) only had 20 episodes. Its star, Pearl White, made a number of other serials, all of which made her a millionaire.

Mack Sennett made 140 films in a single year, 1912.

Contrary to myth, Tom Mix did not kiss his horse in any film; however, he was kissed by his equine partner in one feature.

Milton Berle's first movie was *Tillie's Punctured Romance*. He played Marie Dressler's baby.

The Stockbridge, Massachusetts, policeman in *Alice's Restaurant* is Officer Obie (William Obanheim), played by himself.

The 1946 Academy Award for best supporting actor went to amputee Harold Russell for his performance as an amputee-veteran in *The Best Years of Our Lives*. It was Russell's first stint at acting.

The gunfight at the O.K. Corral was reported in the Tombstone *Epitaph* under a headline that read, "Three Men Hurled into Eternity in the Duration of a Moment."

There were ten Dr. Kildare movies, plus the one in which the young doctor first appeared, *Interns Can't Take Money* (1938).

Both CinemaScope and 3-D debuted in 1953. The first CinemaScope film was *The Robe*, starring Jean Simmons, Richard Burton, and Victor Mature. The first 3-D movie was *Bwana Devil*, starring Robert Stack.

Vitaphone films (Warner Bros.) were the first talkies; they debuted in New York City on August 6, 1926.

The word *movies* was at first not applied to motion pictures, but to the people who made them. The label was given by the early residents of quiet, rural Hollywood to the directors, cameramen, actors and actresses, and others who dashed around on location disrupting everyday life.

The first film kiss was shown in the kinetoscope show *The Widow Jones*. Participants were John C. Rice and May Irwin. It was a shocker.

Walt Disney's *Snow White and the Seven Dwarfs*, made in 1937 as the first full-length cartoon, used 2 million drawings.

Marilyn Monroe's first film for 20th Century-Fox was *Scudda-Hoo, Scudda-Hay*. Her entire dialogue was "Hello."

The first father-and-son team to win Oscars was the combination of Walter and John Huston, for *The Treasure of the Sierra Madre* in 1949. Walter was best supporting actor, John best director.

The black list used to deny employment in the entertainment industry to suspected "red" sympathizers was drawn up in 1947 at the Waldorf-Astoria Hotel in New York City by assembled studio executives. The "Hollywood Ten" who refused to testify before the House Un-American Activities Committee were: Alvah Bessie, Herbert Biberman, Lester Cole, Edward Dmytryk, Ring Lardner, Jr., John Howard Lawson, Albert Maltz, Samuel Ornitz, Adrian Scott, and Dalton Trumbo.

During campaigns it seems as though we see endless footage of presidential candidates. Movies were first taken of presidential nominees—President Coolidge (Republican), Senator LaFollette (Progressive), and John Davis (Democratic)—in August 1924 and shown to movie audiences in September 1924. Photographers were Theodore W. Case and Lee De Forest.

Ronald Reagan's first movie was *Love Is on the Air*, released in 1937. In it he plays radio announcer Andy McLeod. His co-star was June Travis. He and his wife Nancy (Davis) acted together in one film: *Hellcats of the Navy* (1957).

The first motion pictures were shown in West Orange, New Jersey, by Thomas A. Edison.

Koster and Bial's Music Hall in New York City was the site of the first public movie projection on a theater screen, on April 23, 1896.

The price charged at nickelodeons—the first movie theaters—was often a dime, not a nickel.

The first drive-in movie theater opened in Camden, New Jersey, in June 1933.

The first talking movie was *Don Juan*, starring John Barrymore, which opened at the Warner Theater in New York City on August 5, 1926. The sound, however, was not part of the film track; it came from phonograph records.

Rita Cansino made her first film, *Trouble in Texas* (co-starring Tex Ritter) at the age of 17. In later films she was billed as Rita Hayworth.

Rudolf Valentino's funeral was held on August 24, 1926. He died of a ruptured ulcer. Valentino's full name: Rodolpho Alfonzo Raffaeli Pierre Filibert di Valentina d'Antonguolla.

The Marx Brothers' nicknames were coined by vaudeville performer Art Fisher. Their real names were Julius Henry (Groucho), Herbert (Zeppo), Arthur (Harpo), and Leonard (Chico).

Elizabeth Taylor is the author and illustrator of *Nibbles and*

Me, a book about her pet chipmunk written when she was 13.

Lillian Ward was the top stunt woman in silent movies. She filled in for Pearl White in the *Perils of Pauline*.

Ben Kingsley, Oscar-winning star of *Gandhi*, was given the name Krishna Bhanji when he was born.

Ronald Reagan appeared as an actor in 54 films.

Shirley Temple received 135,000 gifts for her eighth birthday.

Early actresses were not identified by their own name; this kept their salaries down. Mary Pickford was known as Little Mary, the Biograph Girl.

Dale Evans was married to Tom F. Fox for two years before she married Roy Rogers in 1947. Rogers's first wife had died.

Mr. and Mrs. Ludlow Ogden Smith, originally from Philadelphia, were dropped from the *Social Register* in 1934 because Mrs. Smith had taken up the unsavory profession of movie actress. (Who was Mrs. Smith? She was better known as Katharine Hepburn.)

Greta Garbo's first spoken words in a film were "Gif me a viskey, ginger ale on the side—and don't be stingy, baby," in *Anna Christie* (1930).

Tallulah Bankhead's father, William B. Bankhead, was a member of Congress and a Speaker of the House.

Fred Astaire's talents were assessed in his first Hollywood screen test: "Can't act. Slightly bald. Can dance a little." He began his career in vaudeville as the World's Worst Juggler.

Greta Garbo did not say she wanted to be alone. She said (she says now) she wanted to be *let* alone.

Ethel, Lionel, and John Barrymore appeared together only once, in *Rasputin and the Empress*, in 1932. It was Ethel's first talkie.

Theda Bara once played a sweet romantic heroine, in *Kathleen Mavourneen* (1919). The film was a flop.

Olivia de Havilland was born in Tokyo, Japan.

Adolphe Menjou's autobiography, published in 1948, was titled *It Took Nine Tailors*.

Errol Flynn's autobiography was titled *My Wicked, Wicked Ways*. It was published posthumously in 1960.

W. C. Fields did not say, "Any man who hates dogs and babies can't be all bad." It was said of him by Leo Rostin at a Hollywood banquet honoring Fields on February 16, 1939.

Music

Stephen Foster, composer of numerous songs about the South and black life, visited the South only once. (Minstrel songs written in what was supposed to be Southern black dialect were called "Ethiopian numbers.")

President Ulysses S. Grant insisted there were only two songs he knew. One, he said, was "Yankee Doodle." The other wasn't.

Music publishers were reluctant to bring out "In the Good Old Summertime" because it would—they thought—have only seasonal appeal. In its first year of publication, it sold 1 million copies.

"Frankie and Johnny" was originally published, in 1904, as "He Done Me Wrong, or Death of Bill Bailey."

Fanny Crosby was the author of over 8,000 hymns in the 1800s.

Yankee Doodle went to town
Riding on a pony
Stuck a feather in his cap
And called it "macaroni."

Macaroni? The reference is to the Macaroni Club, a London club of fops dedicated to bringing "Continental" ways to England. Members of the club dined on macaroni. They also began the fashion for 2- to 3-foot-high pointed perukes, those wonderfully cumbersome wigs.

The original "Yankee Doodle" was written by an Englishman named Dr. Richard Shuckburg, but it was a Harvard sophomore named Edward Bangs who put together the version that has become best known. Bangs served as a Minuteman on April 19, 1775.

At Yorktown, the American armies marched to "Yankee Doodle"; the surrendering British troops marched to "The World Turned Upside Down," which includes the lines,
    If summer were spring, and the other way 'round
    Then all the world would be upside down.

During the War of 1812, two teenage girls frightened away a British landing party by playing "Yankee Doodle." Seeing a boat with British soldiers coming into the harbor, they took a fife and drum, hid behind a lighthouse, and began playing the tune. The boat turned around and left. The two Bates girls—15-year-old Abigail (on the drum) and 16-year-old Rebecca (on the fife)—were true heroines.

"Yankee Doodle" was played after the signing of the Treaty of Ghent, the treaty that terminated the War of 1812.

"Yankee Doodle" was an unofficial national anthem until it was replaced by "The Star-Spangled Banner."

"Yankee Doodle" was the first tune recorded on a record.

Francis Scott Key didn't write the music to "The Star-Spangled Banner"; he wrote only the words. The music is that of an English song called "Anacreon in Heav'n," by John Stafford Smith.

"The Star-Spangled Banner" was first published on September 20, 1814. (It was known variously as "The Defense of Fort McHenry" and "The Bombardment of Fort McHenry.") A few days later, it was sung for the first time. The first person to sing "The Star-Spangled Banner" was an actor named Ferdinand Durang. Durang was in a tavern drinking juleps with some friends and, suddenly inspired, he stood on a chair and delivered the first vocal rendition of the new song.

"The Star-Spangled Banner" was adopted as our national anthem on March 3, 1931.

Stephen Foster was born on July 4, 1826, the fiftieth anniversary of the signing of the Declaration of Independence and the day on which both Thomas Jefferson and John Adams died. He wrote his famous tune "Jeanie with the Light Brown Hair" for his wife, Jane.

Elizabeth Cochrane Seaman, journalist, made a name for herself when she traveled around the world in 72 days, 6 hours, 11 minutes, and 14 seconds, beating the male hero of *Around the World in Eighty Days.* She is better known as Nelly Bly, a name she adopted from a song by Stephen Foster.

Katherine Lee Bates was inspired to write the words to "America the Beautiful" while standing at the top of Pikes Peak.

The words to "Hail, Columbia" were written by Joseph Hopkinson, son of Francis Hopkinson, distinguished Revolutionary War patriot and one of the signers of the Declaration of Independence.

"Hail, Columbia" was first known as "The Favorite New Federal Song." It takes its title from the first two words of the opening stanza. It was set to the tune of "The President's March," a song written in 1789 in honor of the new president: George Washington.

It took Dr. Samuel Francis Smith half an hour to write "America." The Baptist minister scrawled the song on a scrap of paper.

George M. Cohan was born on July 4, 1878.

Theodore Roosevelt's favorite song was "The Battle Hymn

of the Republic." Franklin Roosevelt's favorite song was "Home on the Range." Truman's favorite was "The Missouri Waltz."

W hen the Civil War ended, Tom Dula, of Company K, North Carolina Regiment, was released from a Union prison. He had to sign a loyalty oath before they would let him go. The Union authorities misspelled his name "Dooley," but Tom dutifully signed both ways and went home—and on into immortality. Tom Dula was tried for the murder of his sweetheart and hanged; "Hang Down Your Head, Tom Dooley" relates his sad fate.

The "antelope" referred to in the song "Home on the Range" is not an antelope but a pronghorn, a relative not just of the antelope but also of the goat, giraffe, and deer.

John Howard Payne, author of the words to "Home, Sweet Home," was a direct descendant of Robert Treat Paine, one of the signers of the Declaration of Independence.

The "home" in "Home, Sweet Home" (written in 1823) was John Howard Payne's boyhood home, a vine-covered clapboard house in Easthampton, Long Island. He never had a home of his own. Payne died far from home in Tunis, North Africa, April 10, 1852.

"Home, Sweet Home" was originally part of a drama called "Clari; or, The Maid of Milan," first presented at Covent Garden in London on May 8, 1823. The music to the song was written by Henry Rowley Bishop.

Tin Pan Alley is 28th Street between Broadway and Sixth Avenue, so-called because there were a number of music publishers on the street and all the pianos being thumped on made quite a din.

W. C. Handy, Alabama-born composer and musician, is known as the "father of the blues," a title he earned as the composer of "Memphis Blues" (1912)—the first time the word was used.

Daniel Emmett, author of "Dixie," was born in Mount Vernon, Ohio—in the North. (It took him only a single afternoon to compose the tune—he was writing it for use in a minstrel show the following day.)

Irving Berlin (born Israel Baline, in Tuman, Russia, in 1888) wrote "God Bless America." He originally wanted to use the tune in the Ziegfeld Follies, but he decided it didn't belong in the lavish show. It was first performed by Kate Smith, who sung it on the radio on the evening of November 10, 1938. Berlin donated the royalties for the song to the Boy Scouts and Girl Scouts of America; Congress awarded him a Congressional Gold Medal for the song.

Irving Berlin's "White Christmas" was written for a Bing Crosby–Fred Astaire motion picture, *Holiday Inn* (1942). The song had a particular poignance—it was the first Christmas with all those soldiers away from home.

"I Left My Heart in San Francisco" (words by George Cory and music by Douglas Cross) was adopted as the official anthem of the city in 1969.

Paul Simon and Art Garfunkel went to the same grammar school in Queens, New York. They made their first appearance together in a school production of *Alice in Wonderland*: Simon played the White Rabbit; Garfunkel was the Cheshire Cat.

Casey Jones died on April 29, 1900, near Vaughan, Mississippi. He was an Illinois Central engineer.

Charleston, South Carolina, was the site of the first opera

performed in America: *Flora, or Hob in the Well,* by Colley Cibber (February 18, 1735).

Charles Ives wrote his Second Symphony between 1897 and 1901, but it was not performed until February 23, 1951, at Carnegie Hall in New York. Ives listened to the concert on his maid's radio.

Avery Fisher started his hi-fi business with an initial investment of $354.

Original members of the Dixieland Jazz Band—before it added "Original" to its name in New York in 1917—at its 1916 opening at Chicago's Schiller's Cafe were Eddie Edwards, Dominique La Rocca, Alcide "Yellow" Nunez, Henry Ragas, and Tony Sbarbaro.

Glenn Miller's 1941 hit, "Chattanooga Choo Choo," was the first gold record. When sales passed the 1 million mark, RCA-Victor sprayed a copy of the platter gold and presented it to Miller.

Rudy Vallee started as a saxophonist with his Connecticut Yankees orchestra, opening in Manhattan's Heigh-Ho Club in January 1928. One night he sang instead of playing. Wham!

Bing Crosby's trio was called The Rhythm Boys. They traveled with Paul Whiteman's band until 1929. Other members: Al Rinker and Harry Barris.

"You're a Grand Old Flag," George M. Cohan's smash hit, was originally titled "You're a Grand Old Rag."

Irving Berlin could play the piano in one key only—F-sharp major.

Frank Sinatra's teenage nickname was Angles—as in "knowing all the . . ." In his early fill-in spots on small radio stations, he was paid 70¢ for the gig, to cover carfare.

Bessie Smith recorded 160 blues songs.

Harlem's Cotton Club, the jazz and dance mecca of the 1920s and 1930s, did not admit blacks as patrons. Only the performers were black. Until 1932, a light olive tint was the most pigment allowed female entertainers. This rule was shelved when Lucille Watson, who later married Louis Armstrong, was hired.

Nashville

The first black country music performer was DeFord Bailey, a hunchbacked Nashville resident who played a great harmonica and was featured on the *Grand Ole Opry* for years.

Chet Atkins is called Chester by his closest friends. He traded an old pistol for an old guitar as a boy, and went on from there.

Burl Ives's full name is Burl Icle Ivanhoe Ives.

Ferlin Husky has also recorded under the names Terry Preston and Simon Crum.

Johnny Horton's widow (Johnny was killed in a car crash) was also the widow of Hank Williams.

Woody Guthrie's full name was Woodrow Wilson Guthrie.

Gene Autry's given name is Orvon.

The Smoky Mountain Boys were originally named the Crazy Tennesseans. Roy Acuff, a native Tennessean, changed the name.

The original three Sons of the Pioneers were Roy Rogers (Leonard Slye), Bob Nolan, and Tim Spencer.

Hank Snow was born in Liverpool, Nova Scotia. (He shipped out to sea as a cabin boy when he was 12 years old.) He later became a naturalized U.S. citizen.

Roy Acuff started off as a professional athlete; his career

with the New York Yankees was cut short, though, when he suffered sunstroke during summer training camp (while fishing, not while playing ball). In place of sports, Acuff turned to music.

Johnny Cash's first record was "Hey, Porter," cut in 1955. His first appearance on the *Grand Ole Opry* was in 1956.

Anne Murray earned her college degree as a physical-education teacher.

Nicknames

Sideburns should be called "burnsides." They're named for Ambrose E. Burnside, a Union general during the Civil War who started the fashion of wearing long side whiskers.

William F. Cody got his nickname, Buffalo Bill, from killing bison. He killed 4,280 bison in less than 18 months while providing meat for the workers laying track for the Kansas Pacific Railroad. In 1870, he proved he was worthy of the nickname when he won a buffalo-shooting contest against William Comstock near Fort McPhearson, Kansas. The contest began at 8 a.m. and ended at 4 p.m. In that time, Buffalo Bill killed 69; Comstock bagged 46.

The American Revolution lasted a long time—eight years—and as it dragged on, many Americans began to lose hope. The end was nowhere in sight, and the money issued by the Continental Congress depreciated until it was almost worthless (it made good wallpaper). Disgruntled patriots gave Congress a nickname—"King Congress," which was eventually shortened to "King Cong."

George Armstrong Custer's nickname was Autie.

The *B* in Cecil B. De Mille stands for Blount.

Gerald Ford's name at birth was Leslie Lynch King, Jr.

His parents were divorced when he was 2, his mother remarried, and he assumed the name of his stepfather.

General Horatio Gates, an important officer during the American Revolution, was a timid man. The British nicknamed him the Old Midwife; his own men called him Granny Gates.

The presidential election of 1876 between Republican Rutherford B. Hayes and Democrat Samuel J. Tilden was very close, so close that when Hayes was proclaimed president, many Democrats were convinced that his victory was due to corrupt practices. The new president was nicknamed Rather*fraud* B. Hayes.

Calamity Jane's real name was Martha Canary (later, after marriage, Burk). Her most regular profession was prostitution.

Johns Hopkins University was named for a well-to-do Maryland businessman whose first name just happened to be Johns.

Thomas J. Jackson, better known as Stonewall Jackson, got his nickname at the First Battle of Bull Run (Manassas) when he held his brigade of Virginians against Union attacks "like a stone wall." Before the war, when he was a teacher at Virginia Military Institute, he had other nicknames, including Blue Light Elder (because of his firm sectarian views), Fool Tom, and The Professor.

Thomas Jefferson was tall and had red hair; his nicknames included Long Tom and The Red Fox.

Casey Jones, the railroad engineer whose head-on collision earned him a place in American folklore, was the nickname of John Luther Jones (1864–1900), who was born near the Kentucky town of Cayce—hence Casey.

It was Harry Houdini who gave Joseph Francis Keaton the nickname Buster. (Houdini was born Erich Weiss—he took the name Harry Houdini from the French magician Jean Eugene Houdin, the founder of modern magic.)

George Washington referred to his French friend Marie Joseph Paul Yves Roch Gilbert du Motier, Marquis de Lafayette, as Fayette.

Charles Lynch, the impatient Virginia planter and justice of the peace who has given us his name as a word for meting out summary punishment, didn't hang his victims—he flogged them.

It was the Indian chief Sitting Bull who gave Annie Oakley the nickname Little Sure Shot, in 1881.

Black Jack Pershing got his nickname after serving in a black regiment, the 10th U.S. Cavalry. He was originally called Nigger Jack.

Martin Van Buren's presidency coincided with a very bad financial depression. Many of his detractors took to calling him Martin Van Ruin.

Booker T. Washington earned his unusual first name as a child because of his great love for books.

Casey (Charles Dillon) Stengel was originally called "K.C." because he was born in Kansas City.

James Ewell Brown Stuart, the famed Confederate cavalry officer, is well known as Jeb Stuart. His nickname while at West Point (he had nice hair) was less warlike: Beauty.

The S in Harry S Truman doesn't stand for anything. (His parents couldn't settle on a name.) President Truman was an understanding man, and he allowed punctilious grammarians to put a period after the S.

When American troops first arrived in France in 1917, they were not called doughboys or even Yanks; they were called Sammies and Teddies.

There really was a Molly Pitcher, only her real name was Mary L. Hays McCauley; during the Battle of Monmouth she carried water—in a pitcher—to the thirsty American soldiers.

Paul Revere's family name was De Revoire. His father, a French Huguenot refugee, changed the name to Revere so "the Bumpkins should pronounce it easier." In addition to silversmithing, Revere produced surgical instruments and false teeth.

On the Move

The first shipment of American goods sent to Europe was a cargo of pitch, tar, soap, ashes, and glass shipped from Jamestown in 1608.

In 1815, the journey from New York City to Albany by stagecoach took 3 days—provided the weather was good; the trip from New York City to Philadelphia—at top speed and with no stops—took 15 hours.

Every Wasp automobile (manufactured in Bennington, Vermont, in the 1920s) came factory-equipped with a St. Christopher medal.

The world's first submarine was the *American Turtle*, a one-man underwater craft designed by David Bushnell of Saybrook, Connecticut. On September 7, 1779, Sergeant Ezra Lee used the sub in an attempt to sink H.M.S. *Eagle* in New York harbor. He failed.

The first postage meter was patented in 1902 by Arthur H. Pitney; he further developed it in conjunction with Walter H. Bowes.

Every day, the U.S. Postal Service processes almost as much mail as the entire rest of the world.

The distance between the wingtips of a Boeing 747 (195 feet) is longer than the first flight made by the Wright brothers at Kitty Hawk.

Neither of the Wright brothers ever married.

The first air-mail pilot took off and flew away in the wrong direction.

During the first decade of the U.S. Air Mail, beginning on May 15, 1918, 43 pilots died and hundreds of planes crashed.

Iowa-born Ellen Church was the first airline stewardess. She was hired by United Airlines and made her first flight on May 15, 1930. Church recruited seven other young women to serve as stewardesses. The applicants had to be registered nurses 25 years old or younger; they could weigh no more than 115 pounds; and they had to be no taller than 5 feet 4 inches. The duties required of these slight females included carrying the passengers' luggage, cleaning the plane, helping the pilot and ground crew push the plane out of the hangar and onto the runway; and holding hoses during refueling.

The longest street in the United States is Figueroa Street in Los Angeles, California; it runs for 30 miles through the city.

Contrary to both popular belief and Ford's proud statement that customers could have any color they wanted as long as it was black, not all of the first Ford automobiles were black—some were "Brewster" green with red striping.

Oklahoma City, Oklahoma, was the first city to install parking meters, in 1935.

Many names were tested for the car that Henry Ford ultimately called the Edsel, including Saxon and Belmont. In the end, Ford named the car for his son, Edsel Bryant Ford.

The first Cadillacs, produced in 1903, cost $750—less than the original Model T, which cost $875.

Arthur S. Heineman opened the world's first motel—his Milestone Mo-Tel—in San Luis Obispo, California, in 1925.

Bicycles first appeared in the United States in 1819. The first bicycle in New York City appeared on May 21 of that year; on August 19, the Common Council for the city, cognizant of the metropolis's already congested thoroughfares, passed a law "to prevent the use of velocipedes in the public places and on the sidewalks of the city of New York." Indeed, bicycles did not become popular until the 1890s, at which time they filled the streets and became all the rage, even giving a name to the newest fashion in lip hair: the handlebar mustache. Evylyn Thomas, grasping the handlebars of her bicycle on May 30, 1896, had the sudden misfortune of meeting, head-on, a car driven by Massachusetts man Henry Wells. Evylyn's leg was fractured, and history was made—the incident was the first automobile accident in U.S. history.

T hree years after Evylyn's mishap, a greater tragedy occurred. On September 13, 1899, 68-year-old real estate broker Henry H. Bliss stepped off a southbound streetcar near the corner of Central Park West and 74th Street. Mr. Bliss had barely reached the street when he was knocked down and run over by a car driven by Arthur Smith. Bliss died in the hospital, the first fatality of an automobile accident.

America's first traffic light was put up on the corner of Euclid Avenue and 105th Street in Cleveland, Ohio, on August 5, 1914. It had only two lights, one green and one red.

More cars are stolen in Massachusetts than in any other state.

On the Phone

Americans make more than 350 billion phone calls each year; the average citizen makes 382.

The first telephone operators were men, but they soon proved to be too impatient and quarrelsome for the job. Miss Emma M. Nutt was the first female telephone operator. Hired by the Telephone Despatch Company of Boston, Massachusetts, she began work on September 1, 1878.

Almon B. Strowger, undertaker in Kansas City, was not happy about one of the female operators running the city's switchboard. She happened to be the wife of another Kansas City undertaker, and Strowger was convinced she was switching his calls to her husband. In the interest of fair competition, Strowger invented the first automatic telephone exchange, bypassing the operators.

The first pay phones were installed in a bank in Hartford, Connecticut, in 1889. It cost a nickel to make a call.

The first telephone directory—issued on February 21, 1878, by the New Haven Telephone Company—had 50 listings.

Telephone directory yellow pages first appeared in Cheyenne, Wyoming, in 1883.

People

Frederick Douglass's original name was Frederick Augustus Washington Bailey. His mother was part Indian and mostly black; his father was white. Douglass changed his name after escaping from slavery at the age of 21; he adopted the name of the hero of Sir Walter Scott's *Lady of the Lake*. His first antislavery speech was given on Nantucket Island at a meeting of the Massachusetts Anti-Slavery Society.

Aaron Burr was divorced on the day he died—September 14, 1836.

Rosa Parks, who inspired the Montgomery bus boycott, was fined $14 for refusing to give her bus seat to a white man on December 1, 1955. Martin Luther King, Jr., was pastor of his first church at the time—the Dexter Avenue Baptist Church in Montgomery.

Jimmy Hoffa was 17 when he organized his first union and led his first strike—against the Kroger grocery chain.

Walt Disney mortgaged everything he owned, right down to his furniture, to transform an orange grove into Disneyland. (It opened on July 17, 1955.)

Benjamin Franklin never married. Instead, he lived with his childhood sweetheart, Deborah Read (whose husband's death could not de verified), for 44 years. They had two children.

The 1948 Kinsey Report is officially titled *Sexual Behavior in the Human Male*. Author/researcher Alfred Kinsey was an Indiana University zoologist.

Bernard Pugach hired a man to throw lye in the face of his girl friend, Linda Riss, in 1959. For this, Bernard went to prison for 14 years. When he got out of jail, he and Linda were married. Their book about the affair is titled *A Very Different Love Story.*

Geronimo's real name was Goyathalay. "Geronimo" was a name given to him by Mexicans.

The future U.S. general Douglas MacArthur was dressed in skirts by his mother until the age of 8.

Robert E. Lee did not own slaves (he freed them), and he did not advocate slavery. His citizenship, revoked after the war, was restored to him in 1975.

The man for whom the John Birch Society is named was an OSS officer killed by Chinese Communists at the end of World War II.

Charles Atlas's real name was Angelo Siciliano. He achieved fame after being named the "World's Most Perfectly Developed Man" by *Physical Culture* magazine in 1922 and 1923. Atlas claimed to have once been a 97-pound weakling.

The man who advised us to "Call for Philip Morris" for 20 years was Johnny Roventini, originally a page boy at the Hotel New Yorker. His first Call was broadcast on radio on April 17, 1933.

"Going on the wagon" was coined by Salvation Army Commissioner W. A. McIntire in 1909 when using New York City water wagons to collect drunks on Thanksgiving Day.

Helen Keller was born with all her senses. She was 19 months old when a bout of scarlet fever destroyed her sight, hearing, speech, and sense of smell.

Father Divine's real name was George Baker.

Davy Crockett deserted his wife and numerous children and later racked up an unparalleled record as an absentee Congressman.

Francis Gary Powers, the American pilot shot down in a U-2 spy plane over the U.S.S.R. in 1960, was released by the Soviets in 1962. He worked for the C.I.A. for a while and then moved to Los Angeles, where he got a job with radio station KGIL as the "Sky Watch," reporting on traffic conditions from a helicopter. He was killed in a flying accident in 1977.

Paul Revere's famous ride in 1775 was not his first horseback adventure for American independence. In 1773 and 1774, he made many trips on horseback, riding back and forth from Boston to New York and Philadelphia bringing messages to the Sons of Liberty. When he galloped from Boston to tell New Yorkers about the Boston Tea Party, he put in a bill for his services.

Paul Revere had to borrow a horse to go on his famous ride. He got a horse named Brown Beauty from Dean John Larkin. After the well-known ride, Paul Revere didn't disappear. During the Revolution, he served in the army and faced a court martial for failing to follow orders. When the war ended, he returned to his myriad skills, including the casting of bells.

Senator Huey Long of Louisiana is responsible for the Senate's longest speech. At 12:30 p.m., June 12, 1935, he began a filibuster—it ended at 4 a.m. the following day. He had been speaking for 15½ hours.

Jefferson Davis, future president of the Confederate States

of America, served as secretary of war in the cabinet of Franklin Pierce. One of Davis's ingenious ideas was the use of camels in the cavalry out west.

Just before he took off to put a quick end to the difficulties with the Sioux Nation—just before he led his men into the Battle of the Little Big Horn—George Armstrong Custer took out a $5,000 life insurance policy.

Harry S. Truman served as a captain of artillery in France during the First World War.

There really was a Johnny Appleseed. He lived from 1774 to 1845 and his real name was John Chapman. He traveled across the country, exchanging apple seeds for food and clothing. He used any money that came his way to buy Swedenborgian religious tracts, which he also distributed.

Crispus Attucks, one of the three Boston citizens killed in the Boston Massacre, was black.

Phineas T. Barnum began his career as a spectacle promoter in 1835, exhibiting an aged black woman named Joice Heth. He claimed she was George Washington's 161-year-old childhood nurse; she was actually about 80 years old.

When Phineas T. Barnum was about to die, he expressed the desire to read his obituary, a luxury few men enjoy. The New York *Sun* complied, printing four columns.

Cornelius Vanderbilt never used a checkbook. When he wrote a check, he used half-sheets of ordinary writing paper.

Abrose Burnside was elected governor of Rhode Island for three terms and was senator from the state. He was the first president of the National Rifle Association (1871).

Frank W. Woolworth collected relics of Napoleon and was fond of striking Napoleonic poses.

Booker T. Washington lived the first seven years of his life as a slave. He went on to found the Tuskee Institute and the National Negro Business League. He even invented the concept of "night school."

When he was a child, George Washington Carver and his mother were kidnapped. Only young George was saved—by a posse sent out with a $300 race horse to use as ransom.

George Washington Carver was illiterate until the age of 20. Although he is best known for his work with peanuts, he is also responsible for the development of 536 dyes.

Winston Churchill and Lafayette share a special distinction—they were both granted honorary U.S. citizenship.

At the age of 11, Buffalo Bill Cody worked as a mounted messenger for the firm of Russell, Majors and Waddell; at 14, when the firm changed its name to the Pony Express, Cody was one of the new company's first riders.

Benjamin Franklin's son William was a Tory.

Wyatt Earp, famed lawman and participant in the gunfight at the O.K. Corral, died in Los Angeles in 1929 at the age of 80.

Alexander Hamilton was no fan of dueling—his son Philip was killed in a duel in 1801. Hamilton died in a duel with Aaron Burr on the exact spot where Philip had died three years earlier.

In 1884, two brothers competed for the presidential nomination of the Republican party—Senator John Sherman of Ohio and General William T. Sherman, of Civil War fame. Neither brother received enough votes.

Lafayette's grave is in France, but he is buried partly in soil from the United States. When he left America after a farewell tour in 1825, he took with him a chest full of soil from Bunker Hill, and one of his last requests was that he be buried in it.

No one knows where Thomas Paine's bones are. The author of *Common Sense* and *The American Crisis* died in ignominy in 1809 (people didn't like his book *The Age of Reason*). His bones were dug up, taken to England, moved from place to place—and finally lost.

William Penn believed that the local Indians in Pennsylvania were descendants of the lost tribes of Israel.

It was a black cowboy named Bill Pickett who invented bulldogging (steer wrestling).

Both Wild Bill Hickok and Calamity Jane died in Deadwood, South Dakota.

Adolph Hitler admired Henry Ford; he had a photograph of the American inventor on his desk. Ford, who made numerous contributions to the Nazi movement, had a picture of Hitler on his desk in Dearborn, Michigan.

Giuseppe Garibaldi, Italian patriot and founding father, worked for a while in Staten Island, New York, making sausages and candles.

John Glenn, the first American to orbit the earth, flew 59 fighter-bomber missions in the Pacific Theater of World War II; during the Korean conflict he flew 90 more.

Edward V. Rickenbacker, the World War I ace who shot down 26 enemy aircraft, served as a pilot during World War II. His plane was shot down over the Pacific, and he survived many days on the water before being rescued. He went on to serve as president of Eastern Airlines until his death in 1973.

Julia Child is 6'2".

Bat Masterson, famed lawman of the West, is buried in the Bronx. At age 48, Masterson moved to New York, where he became sports editor for the *Morning Telegraph*.

The British commander at the Battle of New Orleans was the brother-in-law of the Duke of Wellington, victor at Waterloo. Major General Sir Edward Pakenham was killed during the battle; his relative survived the sound drubbing he gave Napoleon.

Performers and Performances

Rock Hudson was born Roy Scherer. He became Roy Fitzgerald when his mother remarried and he took his step-father's name. His agent, Henry Wilson, an inventive and aggressive man, renamed him Rock after the Rock of Gibraltar, and Hudson after the Hudson River.

Mickey Mouse is a thoroughly international rodent. In the Soviet Union, he is called Mikki Maus; in France he is named Michael Souris; in Italy, he is called Topolino; in Japan he's Miki Kuchi; in Spain his name is Miguel Ratoncito; in Latin America he's El Ratón Miguelito; in Sweden he's Muse Pigg.

Walt Disney began his animation career with a character named Oswald the Duck. Oswald flopped, and Disney went back to the drawing board.

Walt Disney got the idea for Mickey Mouse from a very real mouse that he captured and kept as a pet while working at the Newman Laugh O'Gram studio in Kansas City. He named his pet mouse Mortimer and wanted to use the name for the cartoon character, too. His wife thought Mickey sounded better.

Bing Crosby's first musical gig was as a drummer in a jazz band called the Juicy Seven in 1925.

Between 1931 and 1969, Walt Disney was awarded 35 Oscars, the most ever awarded to one individual.

Ice Station Zebra was one of billionaire Howard Hughes's favorite films. He had a private copy and watched it more than 150 times.

The Emmy Awards get their name from "image orthicon tube," a television camera tube. The Emmys were first awarded in 1949; the ceremony was first telecast on March 7, 1955.

Ford's Theater was closed after the assassination of Lincoln, and its insides were torn down. It was rebuilt in 1967 following the original plans. In Lincoln's day, the theater seated 1,700, but with modern fire regulations it now seats 600.

The highest salary ever paid to one actor for a performance in a film was the $10 million paid to Marlon Brando for his work in *The Godfather*. Brando got more than his salary—he also got a percentage of the profits of the film.

Marilyn Monroe's body was the model used by the animators working for Walt Disney when they created the figure of Peter Pan's fairy companion, Tinker Bell.

Humphrey Bogart was born on January 23, 1899.

Most people can recite the names of the Seven Dwarfs, but few know of the many names considered before the final seven were chosen. Among the names rejected were Gaspy, Doleful, Awful, Gabby, and Helpful.

Johnny Carson was born in Corning, Iowa, in 1925.

Captain Video (Al Hodge) had only one Video Ranger (Don Hastings).

The state of Nevada has the most unemployed dancers of all the states; Hawaii is next.

The first theatrical performance in the New World took place on April 30, 1598, on the Rio Grande, near what is now El Paso. A group of Spanish soldiers put on a play.

Soupy Sales claims that he has received 19,253 pies in his face during his career.

Clark Gable's epitaph is "Back to silents."

Howdy Doody had a sister; her name was Heidi Doody.

Elvis Presley's dog-tag number while he was in the army was 53310761.

More actors live in New York State than in California.

Ronald Reagan and Ann Sheridan were originally cast for the roles that went to Humphrey Bogart and Ingrid Bergman in *Casablanca*.

The sole manufacturer of the Oscars—the Academy Award statuettes—is the Dodge Trophy Company. Each Oscar weighs 8 pounds and is 13 inches high.

The first Academy Awards ceremony took place in 1927 and was attended by 250 people.

Elvis Presley owned 18 television sets.

The original MGM lion was none other than Leo the lion, mascot of the Columbia University football team.

Walt Disney is, thus far, the only Hollywood film producer to be honored with a commemorative postage stamp, issued in 1968.

Bob Hope was born in London, England, in 1903.

Place Names

William Jenkins Worth, the man for whom Fort Worth, Texas, is named, is buried in New York City at the corner where Broadway crosses Fifth Avenue.

The name of Modesto, California, means, in Spanish, "modest," or "modest man." In 1870, the namers wanted to call the town for W. C. Ralston, San Francisco financier. Refusing, he was credited with modesty.

Captain Zebulon Montgomery Pike never climbed to the top of the peak that bears his name. A man named Dr. Edwin James did, though, and for a long time it was called James' Peak.

Beverly Hills, California, is named after Beverly, Massachusetts.

The appelation *Dixie* has nothing to do with the Mason-Dixon Line. It comes from the word *Dix* (French for "ten") appearing on banknotes in Louisiana. Dan Emmett's song "Dixie" (1859) popularized the name.

Edward Hyde, Viscount Cornbury, was made governor general of New York in 1702. A cousin of Queen Anne, Lord Cornbury was known to have important connections with the crown, and the New York colonists were happy about his appointment until they first went to visit him. The lord had the habit of dressing up in women's clothes—his excuse was that he was impersonating his royal relative. Dressing up in dresses was the least of his vices, however, and he was soon in debtor's prison, where he stayed until his father died and he inherited the title and returned to England. Lord Cornbury was not forgotten: Hyde Park is named for him.

Hot Springs, New Mexico, is no longer around. In 1950, it renamed itself Truth or Consequences in honor of the game show.

Gary, Indiana, was planned and built by the steel industry, which dredged a mile-long harbor, moved a river, and pumped in fill from Lake Michigan. The city is named for Judge Elbert H. Gary, U.S. Steel's chairman of the board.

In 1644, the Dutch built a wall across Manhattan to keep out both the Indians and the British. The lane running along the inside of the wall became known as Waal, or Wall, Street.

Broadway began as a path leading from the very northernmost tip of Manhattan through the woods to the southern end of the island. It was a trail used by Indians to bring beaver pelts down to the Hudson, and it was known as the Beaver Path. When the trail was widened, people started calling it by a more descriptive name, Broad Way.

The Hawaiian Islands were originally called the Sandwich Islands; they were named for the same man—John Montagu, fourth Earl of Sandwich—who invented the sandwich.

Times Square was called Longacre Square before the *New York Times* moved into the new Times Tower there. The move was made on December 31, 1904. The midnight fireworks in honor of the move started the traditional Times Square New Year's Eve celebration.

"The Big Apple" hasn't always referred to New York City. In 1937 it was the latest dance craze.

Miami was originally a tiny settlement named Fort Dallas, which consisted of only three houses in 1895, the year before Miami was incorporated.

Chicago is derived from an Algonquin word meaning "garlic field."

In 1785, Cincinnati's first settlers named their new home Losantiville. It was renamed in 1790 by the governor of the Northwest Territory in honor of the Society of Cincinnati, a Revolutionary War veteran officers' group.

San Francisco was first settled by Spanish missionaries as Yerba Buena in 1776. The name means "good herb."

An adventurous prospector named Ed Schieffelin wanted to venture into the desolate and dangerous hills of southeastern Arizona. A wise army scout warned him not to go, saying, "All you'll find in those hills, Schieffelin, is your tombstone." When Ed found one of the richest silver lodes ever discovered in the Southwest, he dubbed the site Tombstone.

The name of Abilene, Kansas, was taken from Luke 3:1. In Hebrew, *Abiline* means "grassy plain."

Pabst Peak in Wyoming was so named in 1901. The first two men to climb it sat down at the summit and shared a bottle of Pabst beer while they thought about a name for the place.

There is no apostrophe in Pikes Peak. In 1978, the Colorado legislature formalized the spelling, banning the apostrophe.

Before they were known as the Rocky Mountains, they were called the Stony Mountains.

Alcatraz is Spanish for "pelican."

The name of the section of the Hudson River known as

Hell's Gate does not mean that the area is dangerous—it comes from a Dutch word meaning "clear."

Marietta, Ohio, is named for Marie Antoinette.

Mt. McKinley, the highest mountain in North America, is named for William McKinley. He was not president when the peak was named—he was a presidential candidate.

Twenty-six states trace the origin of their names back to American Indian dialects: Alabama, Arizona, Arkansas, Connecticut, Idaho, Illinois, Iowa, Kansas, Kentucky, Massachusetts, Michigan, Minnesota, Mississippi, Missouri, Nebraska, New Mexico, North and South Dakota, Ohio, Oklahoma, Oregon, Tennessee, Texas, Utah, Wisconsin, and Wyoming.

Anaheim, California, was settled by German immigrants. They named it after the local Santa Ana River with the addition of the German *heim*—"home."

Virginia City, Nevada, is named after an old drunk nicknamed "Old Virginny."

The Indian name for the area that is now the city of Boston was Shanut ("living fountain").

Before it was known as Albany, it was called Beverwyck.

Sing Sing, the famous prison in New York, took its name from the town of Sing Sing, New York, where it is located. Sing Sing renamed itself Ossining in 1901.

Portland, Oregon, was founded by two New Englanders, one from Maine and one from Massachusetts. When it came time to name the new town, they flipped a coin: heads, Portland; tails, Boston. The Maine man won the toss.

Cincinnati was America's first great center of meat packing. By 1830, it was so famous for its hog products that it was called Porkopolis.

John Cabot discovered what is now called Newfoundland in 1497. He named it Prima Vista ("first sight"). It is helpful to remember that Cabot's real name (he was Venetian) was Giovanni Caboto.

Judge Roy Bean, "the only law west of the Pecos River," was so fond of English actress Lily Langtry that he named the town in Texas where he held court after her. It is still there: Langtry, Texas.

Coney Island was thickly inhabited by rabbits—hence its name (*coney* is a European name for rabbit).

The longest place name in the United States is also the longest name for a lake in the world—Lake Chargogagog-manchaugagogchaubunagungamaug. Located near Webster, Massachusetts, the lake's name, in the Indian dialect, means "fishing place at the boundaries, neutral meeting grounds."

The name *Brooklyn* comes from the Dutch *Breuckelen* ("broken land"). The Dutch didn't confer the name because of any physical characteristics of their new home—they named it after a town in The Netherlands.

The Spanish explorer Naraváez, looking for gold in Florida, named an Indian village Apalchen. The name came to be used for the mountainous interior of the new continent, and eventually it became Appalachia.

The original name of Los Angeles—or, the city's full name—is El Pueblo de Nuestra Señora la Reina de los Angeles de Porciuncula—"the village of Our Lady the Queen of the Angels of Little Portion."

It was Washington Irving who, in 1807, gave New York City the nickname "Gotham." He used it in his *Salmagundi*, naming it after a mythical town in England, the inhabitants of which were known for their cunning stupidity.

Because Jonas Bronck, a Dane, had a large farm just north of Manhattan Island, people referred to the area as "the Bronck's Farm," meaning where the Broncks lived. This, eventually, became The Bronck's and The Bronx.

Philadelphia means "city of brotherly love": *philos* ("love") and *adelphos* ("brother"), in Greek.

Many American cities have nicknames, among them:
Akron, Ohio: Rubber Capital of the World
Brimingham, Alabama: Magic City
Boston, Massachusetts: Beantown
Chicago, Illinois: Windy City
Denver, Colorado: Mile-High City
Hartford, Connecticut: Insurance City
Hershey, Pennsylvania: Chocolatetown, U.S.A.
Indianapolis, Indiana: Crossroads of America
Lexington, Massachusetts: Birthplace of American Liberty
Minneapolis/St. Paul: Twin Cities
Nashville, Tennessee: Music City
New Orleans, Louisiana: Crescent City
New York, New York: Big Apple
Paterson, New Jersey: Silk City
Philadelphia, Pennsylvania: City of Brotherly Love
Pittsburgh, Pennsylvania: Steel City
Reading, Pennsylvania: Pretzel City
San Francisco, California: Golden Gate City
Suffolk, Virginia: Peanut City
Toledo, Ohio: Glass Capital of the World

Politicians

Both John Tyler and Andrew Johnson were called "His Accidency" after being elevated from vice president to president following the in-office death of the incumbent.

Henry Kissinger was born in Furth, Germany.

Wendell Willkie did not know how to drive, and he never bothered to lock the door of his Fifth Avenue apartment in New York City.

The first black U.S. senator was Hiram H. Revels of Mississippi, who began his tenure in 1870.

Theodore Roosevelt most emphatically did not want to be nominated as vice president. He *and* his opponents considered it a kick upstairs. (Of course, T.R. then became president after the assassination of McKinley.)

A group of President Hoover's friends, who worked out with the chief executive in the mornings, was called the Medicine-Ball Cabinet.

Eugene Debs was nominated for the presidency while he was in prison serving a 10-year sentence. He was the Socialist party's nominee in 1920.

The first "favorite son" was George Washington—the term was applied to him nonpolitically, as in "freedom's favorite son."

The first cabinet consisted of the attorney general, the postmaster general, and the secretaries of war, state, and treasury. The first cabinet meeting, with President Washington, took place on February 25, 1793.

"I had rather be right than be president" were unusual words for a politician. They were spoken by Henry Clay in 1839 before he made a moderate speech opposing militant abolitionism. The speech was likely to offend people at both ends of the political spectrum and so damage Clay's long-held hopes of becoming president.

FDR's group of closest friends and advisers was called the Cuff Links Club (or Gang). Members of it had been given cuff links by Roosevelt after helping in his 1920 campaign for the vice-presidency.

One of Martin Van Buren's nicknames was Old Kinderhook (he was born in Kinderhook, New York). A New York Democratic club called itself the O.K. Club, after Van Buren. Its meeting of March 24, 1840, ended in a near-riot. From there the term O.K. spread and became a slogan for electoral victory. Other Van Buren nicknames were the Little Magician and the Wizard of Kinderhook.

An American Indian was elected as Herbert Hoover's vice president in 1928: Charles Curtis, senator from Kansas, who was one-half Kaw.

Herbert Hoover coined the term "rugged individualism" in a speech at Madison Square Garden on October 22, 1928.

The first woman elected to the U.S. Senate was Hattie Caraway of Arkansas, who took office in January 1932.

Author Upton Sinclair defeated three regular party candidates to win the Democratic nomination for governor of California in 1934. Sinclair's platform was EPIC—End Poverty in California. He lost in the November election, however, to the Republican incumbent, Frank C. Merriam.

The people Vice-President Spiro Agnew called "an effete

corps of impudent snobs" were the leaders of the Vietnam Moratorium Day protest of October 15, 1969.

Adlai Stevenson served as vice president and later ran for the office again—that is, Adlai Stevenson the first. He was vice president from 1893 to 1897 under President Cleveland, and was William Jennings Bryan's running mate in 1900.

The security guard who discovered the Watergate break-in on June 17, 1972, was Frank Wills, age 24. The five men discovered and arrested on the premises were Bernard Barker, Virgilio Gonzalez, James McCord, Eugenio Martinez, and Frank Sturgis.

One electoral vote was cast for a woman: Theodora Nathan, Libertarian Party nominee for vice president. The vote was counted on January 6, 1973.

The car that plunged into Poucha Pond on Chappaquiddick Island was a black, 1967 Oldsmobile sedan.

The mayor of Dubuque, Iowa, elected by fellow city councillors in January 1980, was Sister Carolyn Farrell, a nun of the Sisters of Charity order.

Rose Kennedy traveled to Ethiopia for a mutual eightieth birthday party with Emperor Haile Selassie.

Theodore Roosevelt's tennis partners, who were also advisers, were called his Tennis Cabinet.

What American politician served as a state legislator, a member of Congress, a governor of two states, a U.S. senator, *and* the president of a country? Answer: Sam Houston. In Tennessee, he was a legislator and governor. In Texas, he was a U.S. representative, senator, and governor. Finally, he was president of the Republic of Texas. Houston was also a member of the Cherokee nation. His well-known Indian name was the Raven, but his lesser-known one was Big Drunk.

The first female presidential candidate was Victoria Claflin Woodhull. She was the nominee of the Equal Rights Party, chosen at that party's convention on May 10, 1872, at Apollo Hall, New York City. Her running mate was Frederick Douglass, the black leader.

J ames Shields is the only man who has served as senator from three different states. Born in Ireland in 1806, he emigrated to the United States when he was a young man, settled in Illinois and represented it in the Senate from 1849–55; he moved to Minnesota in 1855 and represented that state from 1858–59; after living in California for a while, he moved to Missouri and served in the Senate from that state in 1879.

The youngest U.S. senator was Henry Clay, who took office in 1806—when he was 28 years old. According to the Constitution, a senator must be at least 36 years old, but an exception was made for the remarkable young Clay.

Presidential Pets

When he accepted the surrender of the British at Yorktown, George Washington was riding a horse named Nelson.

George Washington was the proud owner of the first mules on American soil. King Charles III of Spain sent Washington two jackasses, which arrived in Boston on October 26, 1785, the first animals of their kind in the New World.

Thomas Jefferson kept a grizzly bear on the grounds at Monticello. It had been given to him by his friend Meriwether Lewis (of Lewis and Clark fame).

Thomas Jefferson trained a mockingbird to follow him around. The bird even learned to take food from his lips.

William McKinley had a pet parrot. The president would whistle the first few bars of "Yankee Doodle," and the bird would complete the tune.

Robert E. Lee's horse, Traveller, is well known; U.S. Grant's horse, Egypt, isn't.

Woodrow Wilson had a pet ram named Old Ike. Old Ike liked to chew tobacco. He didn't spit it out—when he was finished with it, he swallowed it.

Caroline Kennedy was fond of riding around the White House grounds on a pony. The pony's name was Macaroni.

Gerald Ford had a retriever named Patsy. Dog-loving

Americans wrote Patsy letters, asking for her paw print. Patsy got so many letters that a rubber stamp of her paw was made to "sign" her responses.

Dwight Eisenhower hated cats. He gave orders that any cat found on his grounds in Gettysburg should be shot on sight.

Four of George Washington's hounds were named Pilot, Musick, Countess, and Truelove.

Lyndon Johnson's pet beagle, Him, attended his master's inaugural parade. (His companion, Her, stayed home.)

When Taft was president, Pauline Wayne was often found on the White House lawn, munching the grass. Pauline was a cow.

John Tyler had his horse, The General, buried in a proper grave with an inscription.

Zachary Taylor's horse, Whitey, was allowed to graze on the White House lawn.

For Ronald Reagan's horses, 1982 was a bad year. Sinbad, his mount on *Death Valley Days*, was struck by lightning while out in his pasture and killed May 4. Another horse, Little Man, died June 15.

Presidential Relatives

Andrew Johnson's father died when Andrew was only 3. Andrew and his brother, Bill, were sold as indentured workers to serve a 7-year apprenticeship with a local tailor. In 1824, Andrew and Bill ran away; their irate master put up a $10 reward for the return of his property.

George Washington was the third cousin twice removed of Robert E. Lee.

Jesse Grant, father of Ulysses S. Grant, once worked for Owen Brown and lived in his house during the youth of Owen's small son, John Brown.

Warren G. Harding was the first president whose father was alive when he was elected president; he was also the first president to be survived by his father.

Twelve presidents are descendants of kings. Richard M. Nixon is the ninth cousin of Leka I, the exiled king of Albania.

George Washington's mother did not care much for her famous son's politics. She was a Tory at heart and refused to appear at either of George's inaugurations.

Zachary Taylor was a second cousin of James Madison.

Presidential Stature

George Washington had size 13 feet.

James Madison, at 5'4", was the shortest president; Lincoln, at 6'4", was the tallest.

All U.S. presidents have worn eyeglasses. Most removed them in public.

Lincoln was tall and muscular; he had a 32-inch waist. He wore size 14 boots.

James Madison weighed only 100 pounds. William Howard Taft weighed between 300 and 350 pounds—a special bathtub had to be constructed for him in the White House.

James A. Garfield was the only president thus far to be left-handed.

Although only six people in the world knew it, President Theodore Roosevelt was blind in his left eye. He was struck in the eye during a boxing match with an army officer in 1904, and by 1908, he had lost all sight in the eye.

Three presidents have had red hair: George Washington, Martin Van Buren, Thomas Jefferson.

In 1940, the Division of Fine Arts of the University of Southern California selected Ronald Reagan as the possessor of the most nearly perfect male figure.

Printed Words

Christopher Columbus took a copy of Marco Polo's book with him on his first voyage in 1492. He wanted to read up on China, which is where Polo had traveled in the thirteenth century and where Columbus thought he was going. (It was probably the first book in the New World.)

The first work printed in the British colonies (aside from a broadside) was *An Almanak for the Year of Our Lord, 1639, Calculated for New England*, by William Peirce. It was printed in 1638 in Cambridge, Massachusetts, by Stephen Day's Cambridge Press. In 1640, Stephen Day compiled the first full-size book published in the colonies, the so-called Bay Psalm Book, the full title of which is *The Whole Booke of Psalmes, Faithfully Translated into English Metre whereunto is prefixed a Discourse declaring not only the lawfulness but also the necessity of the heavenly ordinance of singing scripture psalmes in the Churches of God.* The 296-page book was also published by the Cambridge Press, Cambridge, Massachusetts.

The U.S. Government Printing Office in Washington, D.C., prints about 6,000 new titles each year.

The first American novel, *The Power of Sympathy; or, The Triumph of Nature Founded in Truth*, was published in 1789 in Boston, written by "Philenia" (probably a pseudonym of William Hill Brown). The first novel written by a black American was *Clotel, or the President's Daughter, a Narrative of Slave Life in the United States*, by William Wells Brown. It was first published in England, in 1853; it was reprinted, with a few changes, in Boston in 1864, under the title *Clotelle, A Tale of the Southern States*.

The U.S.S. *Triton* was the first submarine to circle the earth. It left New London, Connecticut, on February 16, 1960, and returned on May 10, 1960, after traveling 41,500 miles. The skipper of the sub was Captain E. L. Beach, author of *Run Silent, Run Deep.*

Ben-Hur, the historical novel written by Civil War general Lew Wallace, was the first work of fiction to be blessed by a pope.

Sylvia Townsend Warner's novel *Lolly Willowes; or, The Loving Huntsman*, was the first "selection" of the Book-of-the-Month Club when it was founded in 1926.

The first cookbook printed in the United States was *The Compleat Housewife*. It was modeled after a book written by E. Smith in England and was published in Williamsburg, Virginia, in 1742.

TV Guide and *The Reader's Digest* are way ahead of their competition in circulation. *TV Guide* sells 19 million copies each week; *The Reader's Digest* sells 17,750 copies per month in the United States and over 12 million abroad in 15 languages. *National Geographic* comes in third with 10 million copies.

The "Zip" in Zip Code stands for "Zone Improvement Program." The World Trade Center in New York City has two zip codes: 10047 and 10048.

"Laugh, and the world laughs with you, / Weep, and you weep alone" is from "The Way of the World," by Ella Wheeler Wilcox.

Sara Joseph Hale wrote "Mary Had a Little Lamb." Her creation was honored by Thomas Edison, who read it when testing his newly invented "Phonograph" on December 6, 1877.

Public Health

Several U.S. cities have suffered from twentieth-century epidemics of the medieval killer, bubonic plague. A large part of Honolulu was burned out in 1900 when officials set fire to Chinatown in an attempt to control a plague epidemic. Other cities with epidemics were San Francisco, in 1900 and 1907; Seattle in 1907; New Orleans in 1914 and 1919; and Los Angeles in 1924.

The first known successful appendectomy was performed January 4, 1885, in Davenport, Iowa. The surgeon was Dr. William West Grant, and the patient was Mary Gartside.

A suggestion that Harvard Medical School students take written examinations in 1869 was rejected by the school's dean because, he said, "A majority of the students cannot write well enough."

One of the six biggest names in the news in 1835, according to the Associated Press, was . . . Alice Jane McHenry. Who? She was a girl with an inverted stomach who underwent a successful operation.

Grand Rapids, Michigan, was the first U.S. municipality to fluoridate its water, in 1945. It was controversial from the outset.

The Pap test is named for Dr. George Nicholas Papanicolaoa, a Greek-American who developed the cervical cancer test in 1928.

Medical tests for couples seeking marriage licenses were first required by the New York State Desmond-Breitbart law in 1938.

Smallpox inoculation was introduced to the New World by Boston physician Zabdiel Boylston during an epidemic in 1721. When 6 of the 247 colonists he inoculated died, Boylston was attacked by a mob.

The Apgar score (a 10-point checklist for newborn infants) is named for anesthesiologist Virginia Apgar, who developed it.

Insurance company names used to be more graphic. Metropolitan Life Insurance began in 1863 as the National Life & Limb Insurance Co.

Barber poles were originally red and white to advertise the barber's second occupation of surgeon—not too reassuringly; the red stood for blood, the white for surgical dressings.

New Yorkers rioted for three days in April 1788 when they discovered doctors at the Hospital of the City of New York were robbing graves to supply themselves and students with cadavers for dissecting. The doctors were jailed to protect them from the mob. The riot led to the passage of a state law in 1789 allowing doctors to procure cadavers legally.

Elizabeth Blackwell, the first female M.D. in the United States, was admitted to Geneva College (N.Y.) medical school as a joke. She graduated at the head of her class in 1849.

Quotations

Neither of the Wright brothers, pioneer aviators, was given to loquacity. Wilbur provided a possible clue to their taciturnity: "The only birds that talk are parrots, and they don't fly very high."

One of Teddy Roosevelt's favorite phrases was "By Godfrey, isn't that bully!"

On May 1, 1898, the Asiatic Squadron of the U.S. Navy steamed into Manila Bay. As the morning mists lifted, Commodore George Dewey calmly said, "You may fire when ready, Gridley." Ten Spanish men-of-war were soon beneath the sea. The American public, delighted with the victory, fell in love with Dewey's low-key command. There was only one question—who or what was "Gridley"? Investigation revealed that Gridley was Charles Vernon Gridley, commanding officer of the fleet's flagship. (Gridley, already in poor health, died while returning to the United States.)

On May 10, 1775, Ethan Allen and his Green Mountain Boys stormed Fort Ticonderoga and quickly captured the sleepy British garrison. According to legend, when the startled British officer inquired of Allen under what authority he acted, Allen roared back, "In the name of the Great Jehovah and the Continental Congress!"

The first line of the second paragraph of the Declaration of Independence has become famous: "We hold these truths to be self-evident; that all men are created equal." This is not exactly what Thomas Jefferson wrote. Indeed, more than 80 changes were made in his original manuscript of the Declaration. Jefferson's first draft of the well-known

line read, "We hold these truths to be sacred and unde-
niable; that all men are created equal and independent."

On the morning of September 22, 1776, Nathan Hale was
hanged as a spy by the British. A tree served as his gallows.
Before the noose was put around his neck, he faced his
captors, who were standing in a field in front of him, and
said, "I only regret that I have but one life to lose for my
country." The tree and the field are gone—the site of Hale's
execution is near what is now the corner of 66th Street and
Third Avenue in busy Manhattan.

John Paul Jones's ship, the *Bonhomme Richard*, was filling
with water and beginning to sink. The rigging was on fire,
the deck was smashed and littered with dead American
sailors. Surveying the damage, the commander of the British ship called out, "Do you surrender?" Jones is supposed
to have called back, "I have not yet begun to fight!" His
reply was probably much more terse—and much more in
keeping with nautical tradition. "Hell, no!" screamed John
Paul Jones, the tide of battle turned, and the American
navy was born.

"I don't go so far as to think that the only good Indians are
the dead Indians," stated Theodore Roosevelt. "But I believe nine out of ten are, and I shouldn't like to inquire too
closely into the case of the tenth."

Although the statement is sometimes attributed to him,
John J. Pershing, commander of the American Expedition-
ary Force in World War I, never said, "Lafayette, we are
here." He frequently expressed the wish that he had, however. (It was Colonel Charles E. Stanton, a nephew of
Edwin M. Stanton, Lincoln's secretary of war, who made
the statement.)

Calvin Coolidge—"Silent Cal"—was famous for keeping his
mouth closed. His silence was purposeful; he once ex-

plained, "I have noticed that nothing I never said ever did me any harm."

Herbert Hoover, taking office during the Great Depression, assessed the nation's woes: "The country is not in good condition." Hoover understood the problems, stating, "When a great many people are unable to find work, unemployment results."

Although it sounds like some great man's immortal line, "Now is the time for all good men to come to the aid of their country" began as a typing test. It was coined by a friend of Christopher L. Sholes, inventor of the first practical typewriter.

Humphrey Bogart never said, "Tennis, anyone?" Nor did he ever say, "Play it again, Sam."

Radio

Radio entered politics with the administration of Warren G. Harding. His inauguration was the first to be covered in a radio broadcast. He installed the first presidential radio in the White House, on February 8, 1922. The first presidential speech to be broadcast was Harding's dedication of the Francis Scott Key Memorial on June 14, 1922, carried by Baltimore station WEAR.

Soap operas are so called because most of the early radio serials were sponsored by soap companies.

Ed Wynn originated the use of canned laughter, on his *Texaco Star Theater* in the 1930s.

The voice of *The March of Time* (a secret at the time) was Westbrook Van Voorhis.

The U.S. Army's portable rocket launcher was named after a look-alike musical instrument invented by 1930s radio personality Bob Burns—the bazooka. Burns was a comedian who told stories about the hometown folks in Van Buren, Arkansas.

The first radio commercial was broadcast over New York station WEAF on August 28, 1922. It promoted the Hawthorn Court apartments.

The first nationwide radio broadcast was of the 1927 New Year's Day Rose Bowl game featuring Stanford and Alabama and announcer Graham McNamee (who later became straight man for Texaco fire chief Ed Wynn). In case this might be considered too low-brow a subject for the historic event, a second nationwide broadcast that night featured a New York Symphony Orchestra concert.

At the height of its popularity, the Chiquita Banana song could be heard on radio 2,700 times a week.

Crooning was invented by 1920s radio singer Vaughn de Leath, who had to keep her voice gentle so as not to damage or blow out the delicate studio microphones.

The Pepsi-Cola jingle was broadcast 296,426 times in 1941.

Secretary of Commerce Herbert Hoover astutely declared that "the American people will never stand for advertising on the air." Commercials began soon after.

Radio Personalities

J im and Marian Jordan were Fibber McGee and Molly. They lived at 79 Wistful Villa, Peoria. Fibber was originally Smackout, a small-town grocer who was always "smack out" of whatever you wanted.

For the first three years of their partnership, from 1922 to 1925, Gracie Allen played straight man to George Burns. Even so, Gracie was getting the laughs, so they switched roles.

The voices of Amos and Andy were Freeman Gosden (Amos) and Charles Correll (Andy), white vaudeville veterans. The show aired Monday through Friday evenings at 7:00 p.m. EST on NBC-Red.

Kate Smith's theme song for her weekly Thursday night show was "When the Moon Comes Over the Mountain."

Arthur Godfrey was originally billed as "Red Godfrey, the Warbling Banjoist" in his early days on the local Baltimore radio station WFBR.

Jack Benny's real name was Benjamin Kubelsky. He began in vaudeville as Ben K. Benny. His radio show ran for 23 years, first on NBC, then CBS, and his TV show went on for 10 years.

The Green Hornet's real name was Britt Reid. The Lone Ranger's real name was John Reid. They were created by the same men. Britt's father, Dan, was the Lone Ranger's nephew, named for the masked man's older brother, who had been killed in the Cavendish ambush that had turned John Reid into the Lone Ranger.

Eddie Cantor brought George Burns and Gracie Allen to radio as guests on his show in 1931. Another protegée was Dinah Shore.

Groucho Marx began his successful radio career in 1945 when he did a marathon show with Bob Hope. When Hope's script slipped to the floor, Groucho stepped on it, and the show went on, ad-lib. From that moment on, the show—and Groucho—were successes.

One of the performers on *Our Gal Sunday* was Belle "Bubbles" Silverman, who later became Beverly Sills, opera star.

The original host of *Make-Believe Ballroom,* one of the earliest disc jockey shows, was Martin Block.

The characters to be found in *Allen's Alley* were Titus Moody, Mrs. Nussbaum, Ajax Cassidy, and Senator Claghorn, who were joined by Fred Allen.

The regular panel members on *Information Please* were Franklin P. Adams (a newspaper columnist), Clifton Fadiman (the *New Yorker* book critic), John Kiernan (*New York Times* sports editor), and Oscar Levant (pianist).

The actors in *I Love a Mystery* also played leading characters in *One Man's Family*: Jack was also Paul Barbour, Doc was Clifford, and Reggie was Nicholas Lacey.

Cynthia Cline, Gerard Darrow, and Van Dyke Tiers were the three original *Quiz Kids*.

The woman who went on trial in 1949 as Tokyo Rose, the World War II radio broadcaster, was Iva Toguri D'Aquino, a native of Los Angeles and graduate of UCLA. She received a six-year sentence for undermining U.S. morale.

Joseph M. White was a popular radio singer in the 1920s and 1930s. Known as "The Silver Masked Tenor," he appeared in public attired in a sterling-silver mask.

Eddie Anderson played the character named Rochester on Jack Benny's Sunday night radio program. The full name of the character was Rochester Van Jones, but the Van Jones was soon dropped. One of Rochester's duties was to look after Carmichael, the polar bear Benny kept in the basement to guard his vault.

Radio Shows

Rishigan Fishigan of Shishigan, Michigan, was a character on *Vic and Sade*, which was about Victor Rodney Gook and his wife Sade of Crooper, Illinois. Vic was chief accountant of Consolidated Kitchenware Co., Plant 14.

"Red River Valley" was the theme song of *Our Gal Sunday*. Other themes were "Rose of Tralee"—*Backstage Wife*, "Polly Wolly Doodle"—*Just Plain Bill*, and "Funiculi, Funicula"—*Lorenzo Jones*.

Helen Trent, when not pursuing or being pursued by romance, worked as a fashion designer. Young Widder Brown ran a tearoom.

Pepper Young's Family was aired by both CBS and NBC in 1938; listeners could tune in daily at three different times.

Captain Midnight was U.S. Captain Albright, who fulfilled an anti-Nazi mission at the last possible moment—midnight—hence his name.

One Man's Family was broadcast from April 28, 1932, through May 1959—a total of 3,256 episodes. The family consisted of Henry and Fanny Barbour and their five children: Paul (whose adopted son was Teddy); Hazel (she and her husband William Herbert had twin sons, Hank and Pinky); Claudia (who married Nicholas Lacey after her first husband, John Roberts, died—their child was Penny); Clifford, Claudia's twin (his wife, Anne Waite, died the year they were married); and Jack (whose wife, Betty, gave birth to triplets).

When *Amos 'n' Andy* was *Sam 'n' Henry*, the title characters came from Birmingham, Alabama, and their lodge was Jewels of the Crown. As Amos and Andy, they hailed from Atlanta, Georgia, and belonged to the Mystic Knights of the Sea.

The first election-return broadcast (of the Harding–Cox contest) on November 2, 1920, was also the first regularly scheduled broadcast by a commercially licensed station. It marked the debut of station KDKA, Pittsburgh.

The Fred Allen Show began on October 23, 1932, as the *Linit Bath Club Revue*, then became the *Salad Bowl Revue* (sponsor: Hellmann's Mayonnaise), the *Sal Hepatica Revue*, and the *Texaco Star Theater*, before finally being named for Allen himself.

Rudy Vallee opened his *Fleishmann Hour* radio show with "Heigh-ho, everybody!" Vallee learned to play the saxophone through a mail-order course.

We all know how idiotic TV programming is. Do you yearn to go back to the good old days of quality radio programming? If so, ponder these words of Dr. Lee De Forest, an early radio pioneer who invented the three-element electron tube in 1906. In 1947 he asked a broadcasting convention, "What have you done with my child? This child of mine is moronic, as though you and your sponsors believe the majority of listeners have only moron minds."

Radio's "Happiness Boys" were Billy Jones and Ernie Hare, a pair of comedians sponsored by the Happiness Candy Company.

Lum and Abner aired daily for 22 years. Lum Edwards was played by Chester Lauck and Abner Peabody was Norris Goff. Together they ran the Jot 'Em Down Store. The town of Waters, Arkansas, renamed itself Pine Ridge after the Arkansas town in which the show was set.

The *Grand Ole Opry* was first broadcast on November 28, 1925, over WSM of Nashville. Called *WSM Barn Dance*, it changed to its present name in 1927.

The first *Meet the Press* show aired on October 5, 1945, on New York radio. Moderator Laurence E. Spivak continued on the show (it moved to NBC-TV in November 1947) until November 1975.

The radio comedy *Duffy's Tavern* always opened with the line, "Duffy's Tavern, where the elite meet to eat. Archie the manager speaking. Duffy ain't here. Oh, hello, Duffy."

The Lone Ranger radio show was taken from James E. Jewell's *Curly Edwards and the Cowboys*. Tonto's name for the Lone Ranger, Kemo Sabe, meant "trusting brave," and was the name of Jewell's future father-in-law's summer camp.

The soap opera *Ma Perkins* ran for 27 years. Throughout, Ma was played by Virginia Payne. Ma ran a lumberyard in Rushville Center.

The mad laughter after *The Shadow*'s opening line was supplied by Orson Welles.

The famous *War of the Worlds* radio show that convinced thousands of people the Martians had landed was titled *Invasion from Mars* and was written by Howard Koch (inspired by the H. G. Wells novel). Aired on October 30, 1938, it opened with the Ramon Raquello orchestra playing "La Cumparsita," which was soon interrupted by announcements of developments on Mars. The Martian spacecraft landed on the Wilmuth farm, Grovers Mill, New Jersey. Events there were reported by newsman Carl Phillips.

CBS's Professor Quiz introduced the quiz show to network broadcasting in 1936. The Professor's opening question on his opening show was: "What is the difference between a *lama* with one *l* and a *llama* with two *l*'s?"

In order to win the jackpot on *Pot o' Gold* in 1940, you had to name the song being played by Horace Heidt's band. If you didn't know, you still won $1,000 for answering your phone.

The opening line of *Our Gal Sunday* was "Can this girl from a mining town in the West find happiness as the wife of a wealthy and *titled* Englishman?" (The answer, ultimately, was no. Sunday divorced Lord Henry Brinthrope in 1958.)

In 1940 *The Goldbergs* (which ran on radio from 1929 to 1946) was interrupted by a broadcast of Adolf Hitler speaking. The program then declared, "You have heard the concluding remarks of Chancellor Hitler through the courtesy of the Goldbergs."

The "$64 Question" was a feature of the radio show *Take It or Leave It*.

"Rock & Roll" and "Soul"

Chubby Checker's recording and TV appearance started the Twist dance rage in 1961. (Real name: Ernest Evans, Jr.; former occupation: chicken plucker.) "The Twist" first appeared as the flip side of "Teardrops on Your Letter," a number-one song of 1958 by The Midnighters, headed by songwriter Hank Ballard.

The original Supremes were Diana Ross, Cindy Birdsong, and Mary Wilson.

Simon and Garfunkel broke up in 1971.

The radical, political Weathermen group got its name from a line in the Bob Dylan song "Subterranean Homesick Blues," which goes "You don't need a weatherman to know which way the wind blows." The group changed its name to the Weather Underground in 1969.

The Rolling Stones got their name from "Rolling Stone Blues" by Muddy Waters, a 1948 Chess recording.

Muddy Waters was born in Rolling Fork, Mississippi, in 1915 and began life as McKinley Morganfield. He died in April 1983.

The Grateful Dead was founded at 710 Ashbury Street, Haight-Ashbury, San Francisco, in 1965.

Rock star Paul Anka was born in Canada. He made his first million (dollars, not records) by the time he was 17.

Alan Freed, who christened Rock and Roll as a 1952 Cleveland disc jockey, started in New Castle, Pennsylvania, as an announcer for a classical radio program.

Bob Dylan started out at Gerde's Folk City in Greenwich Village. His first LP, *Bob Dylan*, sold a total of 4,200 copies.

George Harrison started the Beatle mop hairdo.

Elvis's first TV appearances were on the Dorsey Brothers show (spring 1956 on CBS) and then the Milton Berle show on NBC—when he swiveled his hips for the entire nation. Elvis graduated from the L. C. Hume High School in Memphis, Tennessee, in 1952.

Janis Ian's "Society's Child" hit the charts when the singer/composer was only 13. She composed the song while waiting to talk to her high-school guidance counselor.

Grace Slick named her child God.

Johnny and the Moondogs was one name the Beatles sang under before they adopted the name *Beatles*. Other names they used in the early days were The Foreverly Brothers, The Cavemen, The Moonshiners, and The Quarrymen Skiffle Group.

Tim Hardin is a descendant of the outlaw/bandit John Wesley Hardin.

Donovan's name as a songwriter is Donovan Phillips Leitch. As a singer he drops the last two names.

Alice's restaurant was actually The Back Room in Stockbridge, Massachusetts.

Members of The Lovin' Spoonful were John Sebastian, Steve Boone, Zal Yanovsky, and Joe Butler. Sebastian was named for his father, who was a famous harmonica player.

The Coasters, whose big hits were for Atlantic, started as The Robins on Spark, an L.A. label.

Almost all of the Everly Brothers' hit songs were written by Felice and Boudleaux Bryant. Phil Everly is 2 years and 13 days older than his brother Don.

Bobby Darin has written movie scores and top-hit songs without being able to read music.

Ricky Nelson's first solo performance was in Los Angeles at Hamilton High School in 1957.

Simon and Garfunkel had a hit song when they were in high school. It was called "Hey, Schoolgirl," and they were then called Tom and Jerry.

B. B. King recorded on the Modern label, on the West Coast. He came there from Memphis, where he was a disc jockey called The Beale Street Blues Boy.

When he recorded his number-one hit (number-one R&B, number-one pop, number-one C&W) "Mabelline" (originally titled "Ida Red") on the Chess label, Chuck Berry was studying to be a hairdresser.

That pelvic hip swivel was first used by Bo Diddley (Ellis McDaniel) before it brought fame to Elvis.

"Sh-Boom," the big summer of 1954 hit that was also the first success for The Crew Cuts, on Mercury Records, had first been recorded in the spring of 1954 by a black group, The Chords, on the then little-known Atlantic label.

Jerry Lee Lewis graduated from the Waxahachie (Texas) Bible Institute.

The original Righteous Brothers were Bill Medley and Bob Hatfield. Medley was later replaced by Jimmy Walker.

Eunice Waymon knew she would upset her mother's religious beliefs by singing in nightclubs, so she changed her name to Nina Simone.

Sam Cooke's first group was The Singing Children, a quartet of family members including 9-year-old Sam. In high school, he and his brother sang together as The Highway Q.C.'s. Later he was part of a gospel group, The Soul Stirrers.

Sex

Dr. William Masters and Virginia Johnson based *Human Sexual Response* on direct observation. Masters and Johnson hail from Missouri—the Show-Me State.

The 1968 Broadway hit *Hair* featured nudity, but the nude performers had to stand perfectly still; nudity on stage was illegal if an actor moved.

A married man is four times more likely to die during sexual intercourse if his partner isn't his wife.

Motels began spreading across the country in the 1950s. They were instant hits. One early motel in Yonkers, New York, reported a 188% first-year occupancy rate.

A 1953 record called "Baby, Let Me Bang Your Box" sold 1 million copies.

The word *virgin* was first spoken on an American screen in Otto Preminger's 1953 movie *The Moon Is Blue*. The film censor did not approve the movie.

Abraham Lincoln said, "Marriage is neither Heaven nor Hell. It is simply Purgatory."

According to the Kinsey report, published in 1948, 70% of Americans at that time had experienced sexual intercourse in only one position—the missionary.

G. Clifford Prout, president of the newly formed Society for the Indecency of Naked Animals (SINA), appeared on the *Today Show* in 1962 with his assistant, Bruce Spencer. Over $400,000 was pledged by viewers to the cause of dressing naked animals before the men quit the game and revealed themselves to be Buck Henry, screenwriter, and Alan Able, prankster.

Noah Webster wrote an expurgated version of the Bible in which entire chapters were lopped out and all dirty words (*teat, fornication, private parts*) were transformed into clean ones (*breast, lewdness, peculiar members*).

The first U.S. obscenity case began in 1821 with the arrest of Peter Holmes for publishing *Fanny Hill*. Publication was finally permitted—too late for Holmes—in 1963.

Slates and Slogans

A"good enough Morgan" is a statement or argument that isn't true but is good enough to be used in a campaign. An unfortunate prisoner named William Morgan disappeared on September 12, 1826, in a case with political overtones. A body discovered in 1827 just before the election was declared to be "a good enough Morgan" until such time as some other body could be more positively identified.

The slate of the Free Soil party in 1848 was called the codfish and cabbage ticket. Nominees were Martin Van Buren of New York, who raised cabbages, and Charles Francis Adams of Massachusetts, a state whose symbol is the codfish.

To oppose the Know Nothing party, the Know Something antislavery organization was briefly formed. It held a national convention in Cleveland in 1854.

The Democratic party was called the party of "rum, Romanism, and rebellion" by Dr. Samuel Dickinson Burchard, a Protestant minister, at a meeting with Republican presidential candidate James G. Blaine, October 29, 1884. The remark probably cost Blaine the presidency.

Andrew Jackson's loudly enthusiastic supporters were called "hurrah boys." Presidential politics had been relatively quiet up till then.

Any New York Democrat who did not support Grover Cleveland's nomination in 1892 was called a Snapper.

Members of the reform movement Good Government

Clubs of the 1890s were derisively referred to as goo-goos.

The elephant became *the* symbol of the Republican party in a Thomas Nast cartoon that appeared in *Harper's Weekly*, November 7, 1874. Nast first used the donkey as the Democratic symbol in a cartoon in the January 15, 1870, *Harper's*.

A "hippogat" is a hippopotamus emblazoned with the letters G.A.T.—Great American Trust. It was created in the 1890s by the Minneapolis *Times* cartoonist W. B. Stewart.

The advice "What this country really needs is a good five-cent cigar" was offered by Woodrow Wilson's vice president, Thomas R. Marshall, to the Senate during a particularly boring debate in 1915.

The slogan "America first" was originally used by President Woodrow Wilson, before President Harding took it up and made it popular.

Political speakers weren't "heckled" in the United States until 1900—before then, the term was seldom, if ever, used in this country. It had been used politically in Scotland for a long time. It was derived from the word for a sharp-toothed comb used to dress flax.

The original "slush funds" were moneys received by the military from selling grease and other trash. They were used to buy items for soldiers that couldn't be budgeted otherwise.

"Dare to be free" was a slogan of the American Revolution.

The word *gobbledygook* was coined in March 1944 by

Maury Maverick of Texas, to describe bureaucratese, or government-speak. Maverick said he may have been thinking of a turkey, gobbling and strutting, and ending with a gook.

The term *egghead* as a derisive word for "intellectual" was first used by John Alsop during the Stevenson campaign of 1952.

The "domino theory" was formulated in 1954 by Joseph Alsop, Jr., the newspaper columnist.

In the 1830s and 1840s the Whigs called their Democratic opponents Loco Focos. The name developed when radical Democrats doused the lights at a Tammany Hall meeting on October 29, 1835, and then lit candles with "loco foco" or "self-igniting" matches or cigars. These devices had been patented by John Marck on April 16, 1834. (The Democrats then invented the term *hoco poco* for the Whigs. It all died out in time.)

A lame duck was originally a bankrupt financier; bankrupts were said to "waddle" out of financial centers as "lame ducks." The term was used politically in the United States as early as 1836.

A kiss ticket or kiss-joke ticket or sugar-kiss ticket was a sheet used to stuff a ballot box. The ballot paper, or ticket, was said to be as thin as the tissue used to wrap candy kisses.

An election story that was false or of dubious origins used to be called a roorback. This was in honor of a writer using the name Roorback, who published an account of slaves being branded with the initials J.K.P. when James K. Polk was running for president. The story appeared in the Ithaca (N.Y.) *Chronicle* in 1844.

Peanut politics didn't start with Jimmy Carter. The New

York *Mail* on May 27, 1887, urged its governor "not to play peanut politics." The term was used at that time to mean petty politics.

Although a man wielding a muckrake appears in Bunyan's *Pilgrim's Progress*, the term muckraker was first applied to corruption-exposing journalists by Theodore Roosevelt in a speech at the Gridiron Club, March 17, 1906.

Station WWJ, Detroit, Michigan, aired the first broadcast of election returns August 31, 1920.

The American term *fifth column* comes from the Spanish Civil War of 1936, when General Emilio Mola announced he would enter Madrid with four columns of troops and then be joined by a fifth column of supporters hidden in the city.

Soap Operas

Soap opera towns and the year the soap premiered:
Pine Valley—*All My Children* (1970)
Bay City—*Another World* (1964)
Oakdale—*As the World Turns* (1956)
New Hope—*A Brighter Day* (1954)
Collinsport—*Dark Shadows* (1966)
Salem, Mass.—*Days of Our Lives* (1965)
Monticello—*The Edge of Night* (1956)
Strathfield—*From These Roots* (1958)
Springfield—*The Guiding Light* (1952)
San Francisco—*Love Is a Many Splendored Thing* (1967)
Barrowsville—*Love of Life* (1951)
Philadelphia—*One Life to Live* (1968)
San Francisco—*One Man's Family* (1949)
New York City—*Ryan's Hope* (1975)
Henderson—*Search for Tomorrow* (1951)
Woodridge—*The Secret Storm* (1954)
Northcross, Conn.—*Where the Heart Is* (1969)
Genoa City—*The Young and the Restless* (1973)

Space

The first U.S. space program was the Vanguard project. Out of 11 attempted liftoffs from December 1957 to September 1959, only 3 were successful—*Vanguards I, II,* and *III*.

The first U.S. satellite, *Explorer I*, weighed 18 pounds, as compared with the U.S.S.R.'s *Sputnik I* at 184 pounds. *Explorer I* was launched on January 31, 1958; after 12 years in orbit, it burned up during reentry on March 31, 1970.

The initial flight of Alan Shepard, America's first astronaut, only lasted 15 minutes and 22 seconds.

The safety of orbital flights for living beings was tested in a Mercury capsule by the chimpanzee Enos (Greek for "man"), in the Mercury-Atlas 5 flight. After Enos came John Glenn.

Astronauts, themselves, named their capsules in the early days of the manned space program. All of John Glenn's family helped choose his capsule's name, *Friendship 7*. On splashdown after the first U.S. manned orbital flight, *Friendship 7* was picked up by the secondary recovery ship, destroyer U.S.S. *Noa* because it was 40 miles away from the primary recoverer, carrier U.S.S. *Randolph*.

Virgil "Gus" Grissom made the second U.S. manned space flight. His Mercury capsule, *Liberty Bell 7*, sank after splashdown, but Grissom was recovered safely. In memory of this, the Gemini capsule for his second space flight was nicknamed *Molly Brown*, after the show *The Unsinkable Molly Brown*. (Grissom died in the *Apollo 1* fire.)

Astronaut (Malcolm) Scott Carpenter named his Mercury capsule *Aurora 7*, symbolizing the dawn of the space age. It also happened that Carpenter's boyhood home had been at the corner of Seventh and Aurora avenues. *Aurora 7* ran out of fuel during reentry, and it landed so far from its recovery ship, carrier U.S.S. *Intrepid*, that Carpenter floated for three hours on his life raft, totally out of touch with everyone.

Scott Carpenter also participated in the Navy's *Sealab II* project and stayed submerged on one dive for 30 days, earning the Navy's Legion of Merit to go with his Distinguished Service Medal from NASA.

The first commercial satellite was *Early Bird*, launched by COMSAT in 1965.

Each Space Shuttle orbiter is designed to complete 100 missions.

The first Space Shuttle orbiter was to be named *Constitution* by NASA, but President Ford heeded the 100,000 letters from *Star Trek* fans and changed the name to *Enterprise*.

The orbital maneuvering system (OMS) of the Space Shuttle consists of 44 small rockets and 2 more small rocket engines in the rear.

The U.S. Space Shuttle's spacelab was built for the European Space Agency (ESA) in Europe by a European company.

Twenty-five experiments designed by U.S. students were selected to be carried out on the *Skylab* voyage.

Astronaut Deke Slayton, one of the original seven astronauts chosen in 1959, was barred from space flight after a heart irregularity was discovered in 1962. Slayton finally made it into space in 1974 on the last Apollo flight, the Apollo-Soyuz Test Project.

The suit worn by Edward White during his historic space-walk (the first by a U.S. astronaut) was made by the David Clark company in Worcester, Massachusetts.

The first black U.S. astronaut was Major Robert H. Laurence, Jr., but he never made it to space. He died when his F-104 jet crashed at Edwards Air Force Base December 8, 1967.

Altogether there were six Apollo missions that landed men on the moon (*Apollos 11, 12,* and *14, 15, 16, 17*). *Apollo 13* (unlucky number?) was aborted when an oxygen tank on the command module exploded and the astronauts shifted to the lunar module and returned to earth. There were six unmanned and four manned test Apollo flights before *Apollo 11*.

The plaque left on the moon by astronauts Armstrong and Aldrin reads: "Here men from the planet Earth first set foot on the moon—July 1969 A.D. We came in peace for all mankind."

Sports

The Tournament of Roses parade was initiated by the Valley Hunt Club of Pasadena, California, in 1886, to celebrate the ripening of the oranges. The first Rose Bowl football game was added to the New Year's Day event in 1902 (Stanford University lost to the University of Michigan, 49–0), but was dropped the next year in favor of chariot races. (The football game was reinstated in 1916.)

The Rose Bowl game became a permanent event in 1916; Washington State College beat Brown University that year, 14–0.

The Stanley Cup began as a $50 (£10) silver cup (it is now a bowl), awarded by Lord Stanley of Preston to the winning amateur team in a Canadian hockey game.

The members of the first All-America football team were chosen by Walter Camp, athletic director at Yale.

Between his pay from the Chicago Bears and his testimonial fees, Red Grange earned $3 million in three years as a pro football player.

Things weren't too good in the professional sports world during World War II. The remnants of the Philadelphia Eagles and Pittsburgh Steelers were combined to form a war-time team nicknamed the Steagles. In hockey, the Detroit Red Wings scored 15 goals in a single game against the New York Rangers and their goalie, Ken McAuley. Baseball didn't fare much better. The Philadelphia team was called the Phutile Phillies. The St. Louis Browns' lead-off batter and starting left-fielder was Pete Gray, who had only one arm. Cincinnati had a 15-year-old pitcher, Joe Nuxhall.

The only America's Cup race sailed in British rather than American waters was the first one, in 1851, around the Isle of Wight.

The America's Cup itself—the trophy—is The One Hundred Guinea Cup. It was renamed in honor of its first winner, the U.S. yacht *America*.

Spalding marketed the first basketball with a female player's signature on it: Nancy Lieberman.

The official state sport of Maryland is jousting.

Babe Didrikson once pitched to the Boston Red Sox in spring training.

The 1974 U.S. National waterski competition featured three generations: contestant Irene Horton joined by two children and three grandchildren.

The automatic Pinspotter patented by New York inventor Fred Schmidt was offered to, but turned down by, the Brunswick corporation before being picked up by AMF and propelling bowling into its position as America's number-one participation sport.

Soccer star Pele had different nicknames in different countries. In his native Brazil he was Perola Negra (Black Pearl), in Chile he was called El Peligro (The Dangerous One), in France, La Tulipe Noir (The Black Tulip), and in Italy, Il Re (The King).

The official name of the World Cup for soccer is the Jules Rimet Trophy.

The Toronto Arenas introduced artificial ice to NHL play, in 1917. The Arenas became the St. Patricks in 1919 and the Maple Leafs in 1926.

Amos Alonzo Stagg lived to the age of 102. (He died March 17, 1965.)

Jim Bakken kicked seven field goals for St. Louis in a game on September 24, 1967.

The United States won only one gold medal in the 1968 Winter Olympics at Grenoble. The winner was Peggy Fleming of the women's figure skating team. Fleming won her second consecutive world title at Vienna in 1967, even though she fell during her freestyle program.

Several Olympic medalists have been pregnant during the Trials, including June Irwin, 3½ months (1952, bronze medal, platform diving), and Andrea Mead Lawrence, less than 3 months (1952, two gold medals, alpine racing).

Wilma Rudolph could not walk until the age of 8. (At the age of 20, she won three Olympic gold medals for running.)

A California to New York running race started on March 4, 1928, and finished 84 days later. The winner of the 3,422-mile "Bunion Derby" was Andrew Payne of Oklahoma, part Cherokee, with a time of 573 hours, 4 minutes, and 34 seconds.

The earliest record of a game being played by white men in America is that of a game of "bowls" played in Jamestown, Virginia, in 1611.

Howard Cosell is a true mouthpiece: he has a degree in law from New York University.

Dueling was very popular in eighteenth-century New Orleans. Duels were fought for little provocation—one was fought to defend the honor of New Orleans coffee.

Football is the only spectator sport that is played exclusively in the United States.

The football jersey worn by Sally (Susan St. James) in the television program *McMillan and Wife* is number 18—Gene Washington of the San Francisco 49'ers.

The 1913 Kentucky Derby winner was Donerail, such a long shot that he paid 91–1.

A horse race at the Jamaica Race Track in New York on May 13, 1931, was declared a false start—after every horse had run once around the track. The one–two finishers of the false start race were Rideaway and Clock Tower; in the rerun official race it was Clock Tower followed by Rideaway.

Eddie Arcaro, who retired in 1962, rode 4,779 winners during his years as a jockey; his mounts brought home $30,039,543 in purses.

Jockey Mary Bacon rode three consecutive races—then, shortly afterward, gave birth to a baby girl.

Elizabeth Arden had rubdowns with Ardena Cream given to her race horses. The winner of the 1947 Kentucky Derby, Jet Pilot, was one of the rubbees.

The first organized rodeo offering prizes to winning contestants was held on July 4, 1883, in Pecos, Texas. The first prize-awarding rodeo that charged spectators an admission fee was held July 4, 1888, in Prescott, Arizona.

Josie Morris of Utah was in her 80s when she captured first place in a calf-roping competition.

Tennis's Davis Cup was created by Shreve, Crump & Low of Boston and given as a prize in 1900 by Dwight Filley Davis, then a senior at Harvard. At the time, it was valued at $800.

Althea Gibson became New Jersey Athletic Commissioner in November 1975.

Only 6 cars (out of a field of 33) finished the 1966 Indy 500. Close to half the field had been caught in a crash during the first lap.

Janet Guthrie drove the 1978 Indy 500 with a broken wrist. (She was the first woman to drive in the event, and finished eighth.)

Stars and Stripes

The first flag to fly in North America was probably the so-called Raven ("Terror of the Land"), a triangular banner bearing the design of a raven, flown by Vikings.

The first American flag to bear stripes actually had only four—representing Plymouth, New Haven, Connecticut, and Massachusetts. It first appeared in 1647.

The original American flag was designed by Francis Hopkinson, a signer of the Declaration of Independence and author of the first book of music published by an American (*Seven Songs for the Harpsichord or Forte-Piano*, 1788, which actually contained eight pieces).

The "Betsy Ross" flag, with its 13 stars in a circle, was not flown until 1783; the legend of her designing the flag didn't begin until 1870—it was started by one of Betsy's grandchildren.

By the rude bridge that arched the flood
Their flag to April's breeze unfurled . . .
What flag? The flag unfurled that April morning was the Bedford flag, a 2-foot-square cornet, which served as the flag for the Three County Troop. The flag had a silver arm holding a sword coming out of a cloud and the words *vince aut morire* ("win or die"). This flag is the oldest flag in the United States.

The United States entered the Civil War with a flag with 33 stars. Kansas joined the Union in 1861, making 34 stars; West Virginia was added in 1863. This flag, with 35 stars, was used during the last two years of the war. Nevada became a state in 1864, thus adding the 36th star.

William L. Todd, a cousin of Mary Todd Lincoln's (Lincoln's wife), drew the design for the flag of California following suggestions of leading settlers.

The flag that flew over Fort McHenry in 1814, when Francis Scott Key wrote his famous poem, was sewn by Mary Young Pickersgill. (The flag is now on display in the Smithsonian Institution.)

The first American ship to circumnavigate the globe (1787 to 1790) was the *Columbia*, under its captain Robert Gray. The ship carried the first American flag around the world, the stars and stripes with the stars in a circle. The ship also discovered a river—in what has become Washington State—and Gray named it after the ship.

Whose broad stripes and bright stars
Through the perilous fight
The flag that Key watched had 15 stars and 15 stripes—the 2 new ones being for Kentucky (1792) and Vermont (1791).

From 1795 to 1818 the flag had 15 stars and 15 stripes. Lewis and Clark carried that flag across the continent to the Pacific.

The flag flying over Fort McHenry, after all the blasting bombs—the flag Francis Scott Key peered at through the morning mists—had 11 holes in it.

The flag of Alaska was designed by a 13-year-old student who won an American Legion contest.

State Facts

The state with the most annual rainfall is Louisiana, which has an average of 57.34 inches. The state with the least annual rainfall is Nevada, which has an average of about 8.60 inches.

Which states claim the fewest resident actors? Wyoming, Idaho, Delaware, and Maine.

Very strictly speaking, there are only 46 states in the United States: Kentucky, Massachusetts, Pennsylvania, and Virginia are commonwealths.

Vermont was not one of the original 13 colonies; it became a state—the 14th—in 1791.

Only 86 miles separate the highest and lowest points in the continental United States, and they are both located in Inyo County, California:
Mt. Whitney, 14,495 feet above sea level
Death Valley, 276 feet below sea level

Kentucky was admitted to the Union as the fifteenth state in June of 1792. Before then it had been a part of Virginia.

William Penn, a good Quaker, had no intention of naming his territory after himself. But Charles II horrified him by calling the area Pennsylvania—"Penn's woods."

The Mississippi was first seen by Europeans on May 8, 1541.

New York State has the highest percentage of land devoted to state parks—9.4%.

Adolf Hitler owned 8,960 acres of land in Colorado. (He had inherited it.)

Thomas Jefferson was both a very inventive and a very scholarly man. He suggested various names for future American states—Illinoia made it, more or less; Cherronesus and Assenesipia didn't.

Alaska is bigger than Texas and California combined.

Indiana and New Hampshire are the only states without mottoes.

Wyoming is known as the Equality State—it was a pioneer in women's suffrage. Its motto is "Equal Rights."

California was not yet a state when gold was discovered at Sutter's Mill in January of 1848. It didn't even belong to the United States. The Treaty of Guadaloupe Hidalgo, signed in February of 1848, ceded the land to the United States, and California—full of gold-hungry Americans—became the thirty-first state in 1850.

The state with the lowest legal age for marriage is New Hampshire, which permits a girl to get married—with her parents' permission—at age 13; a boy has to be 14.

Not all proposed states survived. The State of Franklin is now eastern Tennessee; it lasted from 1784 to 1788. The Territory of Jefferson lasted from 1859 to 1861. It was created in the Pikes Peak region west of Kansas Territory—it became part of Colorado in 1861.

The Great Salt Lake is only about 13 feet deep. However, it is a remnant of a very much larger lake (Lake Bonneville) that was 1,000 feet deep.

Ethan Allen wanted Vermont to be a separate nation, not

part of the United States. Vermont declared its independence in 1779.

Maine was once part of Massachusetts. It was admitted to the Union as the twenty-third state on March 15, 1820.

The Great Salt Lake of Utah has never frozen over.

Over one-third of all Americans live in just six states: California, New York, Texas, Pennsylvania, Illinois, and Ohio.

The most popular street name in the United States is Park Street.

Twenty-four percent of the state of California is classified as desert.

Mount Everest is exactly 29,000 feet high, but the surveyors who measured it didn't think anyone would believe them—the number is too perfect—so they added two feet, reporting a height of 29,002.

The last state to join the Union, Hawaii, is the state with the highest average lifespan for men—73.60 years. North Dakota has the highest female lifespan—80.36 years. The District of Columbia has the lowest for both male and female—65.71 for men and 75.31 for women.

The states that touch the most other states are Tennessee and Missouri—each touches eight.

The two points in the continental United States that are farthest apart are Cape Flattery, Washington, and a point on the Florida coast south of Miami—a distance of 2,835 miles.

The 50 states of the United States average 46,270,000 acres of land each, but they range from vast Alaska (with 375.3 million acres) to tiny Rhode Island (with 0.8 million acres).

Alaska, Texas, and California together make up more than a quarter of the United States' total acreage: 548 million of 2,313.7 million acres.

The lowest state (average altitude 60 feet) is Delaware; the highest is Colorado (6,800 feet).

The coastline of Alaska is longer than the entire coastline of the lower 48 states.

The only state that borders only one other state is Maine.

There are 3,070 counties in the United States.

Texas has 254 counties; Alaska, which is more than twice as large as Texas, has none.

Five of Texas's 254 counties are each larger than the state of Rhode Island.

Californians report the most UFOs spotted; residents of Delaware report the fewest. West Virginians report a remarkably large number—the state ranks fourth in the nation for alien visitations.

The first state to be named—indeed, the first part of America to be named by Europeans—was Florida, named on April 2, 1513.

Before it became a state, Alaska was known as Russian America.

The name of Nome, Alaska, could actually be Name. Since the cape where the town is located had no name, explorers indicated it on their map with "Name?" The *a* was misread by cartographers as *o*, and the area thus acquired a name.

Little Rock, Arkansas, was called—for a short time—Arkopolis.

The second state to be named was California (in 1530). It was named by the infamous Cortez, conqueror of Mexico, and it is the only state in the Union named after an imaginary realm. Indians told Cortez of an island inhabited entirely by women (they were actually talking about Baja California). The story reminded the Spanish explorers of a novel, very popular in Spain at that time, called *The Deeds of Esplanadían*, by Ordoñez de Montalvo, which spoke of an island near the Indies ruled by a queen named Calafía. Cortez took it from there.

One of Delaware's nicknames is Uncle Sam's Pocket Handkerchief.

Montana has three nicknames, including "The Bonanza State," "The Treasure State," and "The Stubtoe State."

Four states have among their nicknames "The Switzerland of America": Colorado, Maine, New Hampshire, and New Jersey. Only one state is called "The Italy of America": Arizona.

Corfu? Corinth? Carthage? Ithaca, Ionia, Illion? Ulysses, Troy, Marathon? They're all in New York State, the state with the greatest number of place names taken from classical antiquity. Other New York names with Greco-Roman heritage: Cato, Cicero, Cincinnatus, Hannibal, Homer, Romulus, Minoa, Medusa, Minerva, and Virgil.

Captain John Smith gave New England its name in 1616. It is composed today of Maine, New Hampshire, Vermont, Massachusetts, Rhode Island, and Connecticut.

States

Connecticut is called the Nutmeg State—not because it produces nutmeg, but because its Yankee settlers were said to be clever and smart enough to make and sell wooden nutmegs.

New Jersey was originally called New Canary.

The U.S. Constitution went into effect on June 21, 1789, when it was ratified by the ninth state, New Hampshire.

The Plantation State is not down South. It's in New England. Rhode Island got this nickname from its official designation: The State of Rhode Island and Providence Plantations.

Connecticut's famed Charter Oak, said to have been 1,000 years old, was uprooted on August 21, 1856, victim of a thunderstorm.

The first state lottery was run by New Hampshire, in 1963. Proceeds were earmarked for education—before the introduction of the lottery, New Hampshire had ranked last among the states for aid to education; after establishment of the lottery, it still did.

King Joseph Bonaparte of Spain fled his country in 1812 and settled in Bordentown, New Jersey, on a modest estate of 1,400 acres. He lived and entertained in his mansion there until 1832. Because of this, New Jersey was sometimes called the State of Spain or New Spain.

Two states voted not to adopt the Declaration of Independence: Pennsylvania and South Carolina. New York abstained, and Delaware's vote was divided.

Florida was discovered by Ponce de Leon on Easter Sunday, 1512, which is the Spanish Pascua Florida, or Feast of Flowers—hence the name.

The first land grant in what is now Georgia was made in 1717 to Sir Robert Montgomery by King George I of England. No settlement was made for three years, so the grant was cancelled. If a settlement *had* been made, the colony would have been named the Margravate of Azilia. Fortunately for Georgians, the colony established in 1732 was given its present name in honor of King George II.

Wisconsin is called the Badger State because its early settlers, many of them lead miners, dug their homes into the sides of hills, like badgers.

Missouri contains at least 2,000 caves, of which 26 are open to the public.

Minnesota is called the Land of 10,000 Lakes. Actually, it contains 14,215 lakes that are larger than 10 acres.

Kansas contains sufficient salt reserves to supply U.S. needs for the next 375,000 years.

Oklahoma is called the Sooner State because its early settlers—the "Sooners"—jumped the gun and entered the territory sooner than the legally designated hour.

Tennessee has been called the Volunteer State. Its governor, Aaron Vail Brown, issued a call on May 26, 1847, for 2,800 volunteers to fight in the Mexican War. A flood of 30,000 answered.

Ohio has produced seven presidents: Grant, Hayes, Garfield, Benjamin Harrison, McKinley, Taft, and Harding were all born there. But it's outdone by Virginia, which produced eight presidents: Washington, Jefferson, Madison, Monroe, William Henry Harrison, Tyler, Taylor, and Wilson. Three successive presidents were born in Ohio: Grant, Hayes, and Garfield; and three successive presidents were born in Virginia: Jefferson, Madison, and Monroe.

Virginia has produced a large number of other states. The original Virginia territory, divided up, produced Illinois, Indiana, Kentucky, Ohio, West Virginia, Wisconsin, and part of Minnesota.

Nevada's status as divorce capital of the United States blossomed after a 1942 Supreme Court ruling declared Nevada divorces valid nationwide.

Six states failed to ratify the Sixteenth Amendment—the income tax amendment: Virginia, Utah, Rhode Island, Pennsylvania, Florida, and Connecticut.

Alternate names suggested for Nevada when the territory was proposed for statehood in 1859 were Humboldt, Esmeralda, Bullion, Sierra Plata, and Washoe. (*Nevada* is a Spanish word meaning "covered with, or white as, snow.")

Three state seals depict seashores—those of Georgia, Oregon, and South Carolina. Two show waterfalls—the seals of Minnesota and Montana. The state seals of Pennsylvania and Oregon are the only ones to show oceans.

The fishing industry is shown on only one state seal—that of Maryland. Two show the oil industry—West Virginia's and Wyoming's. By comparison, mining shows up on 13 state seals, commerce and transportation on eighteen, and agriculture on 28.

The dates on three state seals are in Roman numerals—the seals of New Jersey, Michigan, and Missouri.

All state seals are circular except one—the seal of Connecticut, which is elliptical.

North Carolinians don't seem to mind the nickname Tarheels, but it was coined by Mississippians as an insult: a brigade of North Carolina soldiers failed to hold their position in a Civil War battle and were advised by the Mississippi soldiers to tar their heels before the next battle so they would stick better.

The last state to join the Union before Alaska and Hawaii was Arizona, admitted on February 14, 1912—Valentine's Day.

Arkansas is sometimes called the Toothpick State. An Arkansas toothpick is a bowie knife with a wooden handle.

Utah was first called the Provisional State of Deseret.

Tennessee was called the Washington District from 1775 to 1776. From 1784 to 1788, it was the State of Franklin. It then became the Territory South of the Ohio. It finally became the State of Tennessee on June 1, 1796.

Names proposed for the new territory of Minnesota in 1846 were: Algonquin, Chippewa, Itasca, Jackson, Minnesota, and Washington.

There is no national flower for the United States. In 1889, public opinion favored the goldenrod. The American Nature Association conducted a contest ending on December 31, 1929, to choose a national flower. The most popular choice of the 1,067,676 voters was the wild rose; the columbine came in second. Only seven states did not rank the wild rose number one: Washington, Vermont, Massachusetts, Minnesota, Illinois, Florida, and Colorado.

The Tennessee antievolution statute that led to the famous

Scopes, or Monkey, Trial of 1925 was repealed in 1967. (Scopes's punishment was a $100 fine, rescinded by the Supreme Court.)

Mason and Dixon's line was originally the Pennsylvania–Maryland boundary, named for surveyors Charles Mason and Jeremiah Dixon, who surveyed it from 1763 to 1767.

Three names were proposed when the Arizona district was petitioned to become a territory: Pimeria, Gadsonia, and Arizona.

Nebraska is the only state with a unicameral, or single-chamber, legislature.

The State of Maine was the first to outlaw the sale of alcoholic beverages, in 1851. Prohibition stood until after the repeal of the Twenty-first Amendment in 1933.

Arizona's admission to the Union was vetoed by President Taft in 1911 because the state permitted recall of judges. Arizona obligingly eliminated recall, became a state, and reinstituted recall.

The Klondike, locale of the 1898 Klondike gold rush, isn't in Alaska. It's part of the Yukon Territory of Canada. The gold was discovered by an American prospector, George Washington Carmack.

Some states have strange nicknames:
Georgia: The Buzzard State (there was at one time a very strict buzzard-protection law).
Illinois: The Sucker State (referring either to the fish, or to crawfish holes through which fresh water could be sucked).
Missouri: The Puke State (because so many Missourians flocked to the Galena Lead Mine in 1827, it was said Missouri had taken a puke).

Montana: The Singed Cat State.

Nebraska: The Bug-eating State (because of its many bull bats, which feed on bugs).

New Jersey: The Mosquito State.

New Mexico: The Vermin State.

Oregon: The Web-foot State (because of the exceptional amount of rain in the winter).

South Carolina: The Iodine State (plants that grow there have a high iodine percentage); also the Sand-lapper State (a reference to its impoverished people, who were said to lap up sand for sustenance).

Strike Three!

Pitchers had more stamina in the early days, it seems. Iron Man Joe McGinnity was an underhand pitcher for the Giants who could stay on the mound through both games of a doubleheader. In the first World Series, in 1903, Deacon Phillippe of the Pirates pitched his team to victory in three out of the first four games. And in 1905, Christy Mathewson hurled three Series shutouts.

Denton True "Cy" Young pitched for: Cleveland Indians, 1890–98; St. Louis Cardinals, 1899–1900; Boston Red Sox, 1901–08; Cleveland, 1909–11; Boston Braves, 1912.

Members of the New York Knickerbocker Club, the earliest organized baseball team, wore blue wool pants, white flannel shirts, and straw hats. After each game they changed into formal attire for the postgame dinner.

The Knickerbockers played a game against another pioneer baseball club, the New Yorks, on June 19, 1846, in Hoboken, New Jersey. The Knicks lost, 23–1. In the course of the game, player J. W. Davis was fined 6¢ for swearing.

The tearing down of Ebbets Field began on February 23, 1960. In its place an apartment complex was built.

In their first season—1962—the New York Mets lost three out of every four of their games. The fans were delighted; attendance for the season was close to one million.

For one month in 1963, umpires in the National League

enforced a rule requiring the pitcher to wait one second between windup and delivery. The ensuing storm of protest induced the Rules Committee to cancel the rule.

No perfect games were pitched during the regular season from 1922 until 1964, when Jim Bumning of the Philadelphia Phillies hurled one against the New York Mets on June 21. Jim "Catfish" Hunter of the Oakland A's pitched the American League's first perfect game since 1922 on May 8, 1968.

Evangelist Billy Sunday was a Chicago White Sox pitcher before turning to his new profession.

The "Louisville Slugger" baseball bat was made by the Hillerich and Bradsby company for Peter "The Gladiator" Browning of the Louisville Eclipse, in 1884.

The earliest baseball cards were included in packs of cigarettes. Famed shortstop Honus Wagner would not permit his picture to be included because he did not want to promote smoking by kids.

The first female baseball umpire, Bernice Gera, worked one game (in 1969) and then quit.

The Boston team that later moved to Milwaukee in 1953 (to start the geographic expansion of major-league baseball) was called the Beaneaters, the Triumvirs, the Doves, and the Rustlers before settling down as the Braves in 1912.

The first president to toss out the season's opening baseball was William Howard Taft, on April 14, 1910, at the Washington–Philadelphia American League game.

There *is* a female major-league play-by-play announcer. She is Mary Shane, for the Chicago White Sox.

Mickey Mantle set an American League strikeout record (111 in only 96 games) in his first season with the Yankees, 1951.

The lights for the first major-league baseball game played at night were turned on by President Franklin Roosevelt in Washington, D.C. The game was played on May 14, 1935, at Crosley Field in Cincinnati.

Joe DiMaggio's batting average never fell below .300.

Babe Ruth was struck out on April 2, 1931, by the Chattanooga pitcher Jackie Mitchell, professional baseball's first female hurler.

Ted Williams began his professional career with the San Diego Padres when he was 16 years old. He played 19 seasons for the BoSox. Williams hit a homer in his last at-bat in his last game.

Joan Whitney Payson, owner of the New York Mets, wanted to call her team the Meadowlarks.

New York was the last city to allow daily broadcasting of major-league games. Mel Allen inaugurated the broadcasts in 1939.

Some early baseball rules: Runs were called "aces." The first team to score 21 aces won the game. If a ball was caught on the first bounce, the batter was out. Pitching was underhand only. Umpires sat near first base formally dressed, under an umbrella. Until 1887, batters could specify whether they'd be pitched a high or low ball.

Babe Ruth hit his last home run against the Pittsburgh Pirates on May 25, 1935. Babe was then playing for the Boston Braves. His last game with the New York Yankees was played on September 24, 1934.

Opening day at the new Polo Grounds in New York, August 19, 1917, brought the arrest of John McGraw, manager of the New York Giants, and his counterpart, Christy Mathewson of the Cincinnati Reds. They had violated a blue law banning ball games on Sundays.

On May 2, 1917, a double no-hit game was played for nine innings, the first in the majors. Pitchers were Fred Toney of the Cincinnati Reds and Jim Vaughn of the Chicago Cubs. When the game went into the tenth inning, Cincinnati won, 1–0.

Graham McNamee did the first play-by-play broadcast of a World Series game on October 5, 1921, over radio WJZ, Newark, New Jersey. The game, between the Giants and Yankees, was played at the Polo Grounds.

The first tie for the National League pennant occurred in 1946, when the Brooklyn Dodgers and the St. Louis Cardinals had identical records of 96 wins and 58 losses. St. Louis won the playoff.

The World Series was not played in 1904 because the National League manager, John McGraw of the New York Giants, was angry at Ban Johnson, president of the American League. Johnson had castigated McGraw for jumping to the National League in 1903, so the New York manager refused to allow his team to play the American League champions, Boston.

Before becoming manager of the Giants, McGraw was renowned as one of the nastiest players in what was at the time a dirty, rough game. Until the American League was formed in 1901, few ladies attended major-league baseball games because of the foul language the players lavished on one another. (Ban Johnson's American League promised clean baseball.) One of the first clean players was Christy Mathewson of the Giants, a college graduate (Bucknell) who never played ball on Sundays.

When Maury Wills of the L.A. Dodgers stole 104 bases in 165 games in 1962, he broke Ty Cobb's 1915 major-league record.

Christy Mathewson's first season with the N.Y. Giants in 1900 was so bad, he was sold to the Cincinnati Red Stockings. He returned to the Giants for the 1903 season.

Robert L. Ripley—famous for his "Believe It or Not!" series—originally wanted to be a professional baseball player. He was signed by the New York Giants, but he had to give up baseball when he broke his arm pitching. He began drawing sports cartoons, and, while looking for exciting subjects, hit upon strange facts.

Fidel Castro pitched—he is a lefty—for the Havana University baseball team. He was given a tryout by the Washington Senators (now the Minnesota Twins) baseball team. They turned him down.

George Steinbrenner claims that the Yankees use 1,750 baseballs every season.

The Pittsburgh Pirates were first known as the Nationals. They got their new name from their president, J. Palmer O'Neill, called "Pirate" O'Neill because he stole players away from other teams. They were called the Nationals until they became the Pirates during the rivalries between the two major leagues in the 1890s.

The first five members of the Baseball Hall of Fame (1936) were Ty Cobb, Babe Ruth, Honus Wagner, Christy Mathewson, and Walter Johnson.

The original name of the Brooklyn Dodgers was Trolley Dodgers, a reference to the fact that Brooklyn was a city full of trolley cars, making pedestrianism perilous.

Symbols

It was George Washington who, on April 7, 1782, instituted the military decoration known as the Purple Heart. It was originally called the Badge of Military Merit.

Congressional committees sometimes take a long time to reach a decision. It took six years and three special committees before Congress finally, in 1782, approved the design of the Great Seal of the United States.

The first proposed Great Seal, designed by Benjamin Franklin, had a biblical motif. It depicted Moses dividing the waters of the Red Sea, allowing the Israelites to escape the pursuing Pharoah. The inscription, taken from the Old Testament, read: "Rebellion against tyranny is obedience to God." Franklin's design was rejected, and another committee was formed.

The first use of the Great Seal of the United States was on a document authorizing a prisoner-of-war exchange treaty with the British.

The Great Seal of the Confederacy, designed in England, never saw any use—it was intercepted by Union blockade ships. It featured a wreath of agricultural goods draped around George Washington, a reminder of the Southern heritage.

Rutherford B. Hayes was the first president to use the presidential seal.

There are no religious references in the Constitution. The document doesn't even mention God.

"I pledge allegiance to my flag and the republic for which it stands—one nation indivisible—with liberty and justice for all." That is how the Pledge of Allegiance read when it first appeared, in *The Youth's Companion*, on September 8, 1892. In 1923, "my flag" became "the flag of the United States of America"; in 1954, President Eisenhower added "under God."

Cartoonist Thomas Nast is credited with creating the popular image of Santa Claus. He based Santa Claus on a jolly, bearded fellow named Pelze-Nicol ("fur-clad Nicholas"), a character from the folklore of his native Bavaria.

During World War II, a certain James J. Kilroy had the job of inspecting ships and crates of equipment bound for Europe. Most inspectors marked examined articles with a simple slash of chalk, but Kilroy wrote, "Kilroy was here." When the items reached Europe, curious G.I.s wondered just who this Kilroy was. The phrase caught on, and the words "Kilroy was here" began appearing on walls throughout Europe. Kilroy always seemed to be one step ahead of the advancing American soldiers.

"Neither snow, nor rain, nor heat, nor gloom of night stays these couriers from the swift completion of their appointed rounds." The motto of the U.S. Postal Service is a rewording of a passage written in approximately 430 B.C. by the Greek historian Herodotus. Herodotus was praising Persian messengers.

While George III was being crowned king of England, one of the largest jewels in the crown fell out. Later, after the loss of the American colonies, many Englishmen believed the event had been portentous.

The Baltimore oriole was named by Carolus Linnaeus (the Swedish botanist who instituted the binomial system of nomenclature to classify plants and animals). The bird's colors, orange and black, correspond to the family colors of Lord Baltimore, original founder of the colony.

It was Thomas Paine who suggested the final name for the new nation: the United States of America.

Tennis, Anyone?

Shorts were introduced to women's big-time tennis in 1933 by Helen Hull Jacobs, playing at Forest Hills. Alice Marble followed later that year in briefer shorts at Wimbledon, and soon shorts or short skirts became accepted attire for women players. Women, incidentally, were expected to play in rigid corsets until around 1920.

Tracy Austin was featured on the cover of *World Tennis* at the age of 4.

Ora Washington of the black American Tennis Association was undefeated for 12 years—from 1924 to 1936—much longer than any other female player, white or black.

Gussie Moran's lace panties, which shocked Wimbledon in 1949, were designed by Ted Tinling, a fashion designer who was also a tennis fan.

May Sutton, a tennis champion since 1904, broke her leg and dislocated her playing-arm elbow during a 1930 match at Forest Hills. Not wanting to default, she finished the match propped on a crutch, racquet in the opposite hand.

The backhand stroke in tennis was developed by left-handed champion Bertha Townsend in 1886.

Theater & Show Biz

The Booth brothers—Edwin, John Wilkes, and Junius Brutus, Jr.—gave only one performance together during their careers—a benefit staging of *Julius Ceasar,* November 25, 1864, in which they played, respectively, Brutus, Marc Antony, and Cassius.

The Black Crook introduced the "girlie show" to the United States. Featuring 50 chorus girls, it opened on September 12, 1866, and ran for 475 performances.

Famed turn-of-the-century actress Mrs. Fiske started out as child actress Minnie Maddern.

Profanity arrived on Broadway in 1909 when the word *goddam* was spoken aloud in *The City.*

Actress Olga Nethersole was arrested by New York police after her shocking play *Sapho* opened in the year 1900. A stunned audience had watched Nethersole's stage lover carry her up a flight of stairs and into a bedroom; after an interval of darkness, the lover descended the stairs in what was clearly morning light. This was far and away the most sexually explicit stage drama seen in the United States up to that time. (A jury acquitted Nethersole and *Sapho* reopened.)

"That's all there is, there isn't any more" is a line spoken by Ethel Barrymore in the play *Sunday.*

Gladys Smith's stage name was first used on playbills for her appearance in *The Warrens of Virginia* in 1907. She was billed as Mary Pickford.

John Barrymore performed in only one musical—*A Stubborn Cinderella*, staged in 1909. His co-star was Sallie Fisher.

George M. Cohan's first starring role was in *Little Johnny Jones*, in 1904.

Flo Ziegfeld's requirements for the ideal female figure were a bust of 36, a waist of 26, and hips of 38. The hips were especially important.

Buster Keaton performed with his parents in the vaudeville act called The Three Keatons. Buster's role was The Human Mop.

Calling themselves the worst act in vaudeville, The Cherry Sisters always performed behind a net as protection from overripe fruit and vegetables flung at them by their audience.

Mae West was sentenced to 10 days in jail for her starring performance in the 1926 play *Sex*. Undaunted, she wrote a play called *Pleasure Man*. After its second performance in 1928, the entire cast was arrested.

Harvey, the play about Elwood Doud and the invisible rabbit, first opened in 1944 and starred Frank Fay and Josephine Hull.

Oklahoma! began as the 1931 play *Green Grow the Lilacs*, starring Franchot Tone and June Walker.

One of the stars of *The Barrets of Wimpole Street*, a hit play of 1931 also starring Katharine Cornell, was Flush, a spaniel who achieved great fame.

South Pacific, which opened on April 7, 1949, was still playing to sold-out houses in the second year of its run. Its advance ticket sales were the biggest ever. It also won a Pulitzer Prize.

The first original-cast recording of a Broadway show was *Oklahoma!* More than one million copies of the album were sold.

Vivien Leigh's first musical performance was in the 1963 show *Tovarich*.

When the World Series was shown on TV for the first time, in 1947, business at Broadway's theaters fell off 50%.

The American Shakespeare Theater in Stratford, Connecticut, was founded by Laurence Langner and Armina Marshall, who also started the Westport Country Playhouse.

Nina Hirschfeld was born in 1943. Her father, Al, immediately began slipping her name into his theater caricatures in the *New York Times* and continues to do so.

Tom Thumb, the midget who catapulted P. T. Barnum to success, was given his name by Queen Victoria. When he began his career with Barnum in 1842 at the age of 4, his name was Charles Sherwood Stratton. He grew to a full height of only 40 inches. His wife was Mercy Bump.

In the early 1900s, women's legs were often called Frankie Baileys, after the actress of the same name with a celebrated pair of perfectly formed legs.

Sally Rand, the renowned fan dancer, borrowed her stage name from a Rand–McNally atlas. (Her original name was Helen Beck.) She was a silent-film actress before she discovered fan dancing.

Stripper Sherry Britton was such a popular World War II pin-up girl that President Franklin Roosevelt made her an honorary brigadier general.

Eng and Chang, Siamese twins who toured with P. T. Barnum's show, were attached at the abdomen. In 1943, they married sisters Adelaide and Sallie Yates; the four of them had a total of 21 children.

Little Egypt's real name was Fahrida Mahszar.

Tickets for Jenny Lind's first U.S. concert, at Castle Garden in New York, 1850, were auctioned off for $225. After her success in New York, tickets cost $625 at auction in Boston. Lind made a nine-month tour of the United States, sponsored by P. T. Barnum. She grossed $176,675 and Barnum $535,486.

Liberace's full name is Wladziu Valentino Liberace.

Trade Names

Life Savers were invented by Clarence A. Crane, a Cleveland, Ohio, candy manufacturer. He had a local pharmaceutical manufacturer make the hard candies for him on a pill-making machine and came up with a catchy slogan: "Crane's Peppermint Life Savers—5¢—For That Stormy Breath." In 1913, he sold the rights to the candy, but it's just as well he did, for his son was not interested in the candy business—Hart Crane was a poet.

Dubble Bubble gum was originally called Blibber Blubber.

It was Teddy Roosevelt who gave Maxwell House Coffee its advertising slogan. While dining at the famous Hermitage, the old home of Andrew Jackson in Nashville, Tennessee, he was asked if he wanted more coffee. "Dee-lighted!" responded Teddy with characteristic enthusiasm. "It's good to the last drop!"

Before 1933, 7-Up was called Lithiated Lemon.

Tupperware was started in 1945 by Earl W. Tupper.

Bags of coffee bound for the Arbuckle Brothers, coffee merchants in New York, were marked AB NY. When a brand name was needed for their coffee, the Arbuckles fiddled with the letters on the bags, added a *u*, and came up with Yuban.

Camel was the world's first blended cigarette, in 1913. The camel on the package was modeled after Old Joe, a camel that was part of the 1913 Barnum and Bailey circus.

At the tender age of 9, Hector Boiardi began working in

restaurant kitchens in his native Italy. He was soon a chef and worked in many well-known restaurants in Rome, Paris, and New York. When he opened his own restaurant in Cleveland, Ohio, he made a big hit with his special spaghetti sauce and decided to market it. The labels of his product serve as a pronunciation guide to his name: Chef Boy-Ar-Dee.

The balloon-covered package that Wonder Bread comes in was inspired by the mass of balloons released into the air at the start of the Indianapolis 500 race.

In 1878, Procter & Gamble had a popular product called White Soap which was white and "pure" and did a good job of competing with the more expensive imported white Castile soap. One day, some workmen mixing up batches of White Soap took a leisurely lunch hour and left a vat of the soap churning too long, beating air into the mixture. Hoping that no one would notice, they shipped out the overly mixed soap along with the regular soap. Only when the company received a deluge of letters from delighted consumers did they realize what had happened: the overly mixed soap floated. Harley T. Procter, son of one of the company's founders, decided that this floating soap needed a new name and set about looking for one. For weeks he sought this special name, and then, one Sunday morning, sitting in church and lost in his contemplation, the words of the minister—reading from Psalms 45:8—came through to him: "All thy garments smell of myrrh, and aloes, and cassia, out of the ivory palaces, whereby they have made thee glad." The new product got its name—Ivory Soap.

Old Forester was the first bottled American whiskey, in 1870.

Leo Hirschfield, born in Austria, came to America to make candy. Following a European recipe, he hand rolled and wrapped his candies, and—in 1896—sold them for one penny each. He named his candy after his little daughter, Clara, whom he had nicknamed "Tootsie"—the Tootsie Roll.

Sanka is a contraction of the French phrase *sans caffeine*.

In 1887, a grocer in Minnesota named P. J. Towle came up with an inexpensive pancake syrup made of a blend of maple and sugar-cane syrups. He originally wanted to name it after his boyhood hero, Abraham Lincoln, but finally settled on Log Cabin Syrup, named for the log cabin of Lincoln's youth.

The soft drink Dr. Pepper is named after the father of the sweetheart of its inventor. It might have been better to call it Dr. Pepper's Daughter, after the true source of its inspiration.

Sara Lee baked goods, introduced in 1949, are named after founder Charles Lubin's daughter.

The Shakey's pizza chain was founded by Sherwood "Shakey" Johnson and Edward Plummer. They each put up $850 to open a pizzeria in Sacramento, California.

The model for the Sun-Maid Raisin trademark—the sunbonneted girl holding a basket of grapes—was Lorraine Collett Petersen, who died in 1983 at the age of 90.

The Chiquita Banana song, introduced in 1944, was sung by Patti Clayton. Music was by Len McKenzie, lyrics by Garth Montgomery.

Campbell's soups have red and white labels because those are the colors of Cornell's football team. Campbell adopted the colors in 1898.

The Uneeda Biscuit boy, suited up in oilskins and clutching a box of Uneedas, was Gordon Stile.

Barnum's Animal Crackers had a white string on top so the box could be hung on a Christmas tree—the crackers were first marketed at Christmastime in 1902.

In May of 1886, 53-year-old former Confederate officer John S. Pemberton made a great discovery. The gray-bearded Atlanta druggist was trying to create a new beverage. He already made something called French Wine Coca—Ideal Brain Tonic, but he wanted to make a non-alcoholic drink. His moment of inspiration came when he decided to mix together the extract of the African kola nut with coca extract (the kola nut was a stimulant brought from Africa by slaves; the coca extract, like cocaine, was a derivative of coca leaves). The result was Coca-Cola, a potent brew immediately popular at local drugstore soda fountains and destined to be the world's favorite soft drink, eagerly bought up in more than 135 countries.

H. E. Hires was a druggist in Philadelphia. He and his wife went to New Jersey on their honeymoon. While in New Jersey, Hires tasted an herb tea that he liked very much. Back home in Philadelphia, Hires mixed together roots, bark, and berries and named the concoction Hires Herb Tea. The president of Columbia University, a friend of Hires's, thought the name was awkward and, since Philadelphia is known for its beer drinkers, suggested a change. Hires Root Beer, first marketed in 1866, was the result.

Like Coca-Cola, Pepsi-Cola was invented by a druggist in the South. Caleb B. Brabham invented the new beverage in New Bern, North Carolina, in 1893. Like Coca-Cola, it was a cola beverage. A Supreme Court decision, in 1920, was necessary to allow the Coca-Cola Company to call its product "Coke."

Noxema skin cream was originally called Dr. Bunting's Sunburn Remedy. *Noxema* comes from "knocks eczema."

Oreo cookies have always been round, but when they were first produced they were not flat—they were slightly mound-shaped. The name *Oreo* comes from a Greek word for "hill."

The Baby Ruth candy bar was originally called Kandy Kate. Its new name has nothing to do with the famed slugger Babe Ruth: it was named in honor of President Grover Cleveland's first daughter, born October 3, 1891, who was known as "Baby Ruth." (Ruth died January 7, 1904.)

During the 1830s, the Reverend Sylvester W. Graham lectured across the country, promoting Grahamism, a kind of health-food regimen. Fervently interested in bowel regularity—newspapers nicknamed him "the peristaltic persuader"—the Reverend Graham wanted people to spurn all meats, condiments, white bread, and alcoholic beverages and eat only fruits and vegetables—and his special crackers made of coarse whole wheat flour, which were supposed to aid digestion while curing alcoholism. Graham crackers and graham flour are still with us.

M&M's candies get their name from the initials of Forrest Mars, Sr., and his associate Bruce Murrie. The small candies were first produced in 1940 and were adopted by the U.S. Army because their sugar coating kept them from melting, and that helped keep all those trigger fingers dry.

Dr. Harvey Kellogg acted as director of the Battle Creek Sanatorium, a health-food clinic where everyone ate a lot of bran and teeth-cleaning crackers like zwieback. When one of his "patients"—who had broken her false teeth—asked for something easier to chew, Dr. Kellogg invented a cereal made of crisp flakes of ground corn—Kellogg's Corn Flakes ("The sweet heart of the corn") first went on the market in 1907.

Devil Dogs get their name from the fact that they are made of devil's food cake and are shaped like a hot-dog bun.

The beverage called Moxie was originally called Moxie Nerve Food.

C. W. Post began marketing his coffee substitute called Postum in 1895. One of his early advertising slogans was "Postum—it makes red blood." In 1897, Post introduced America's first cold breakfast cereal, Grape-Nuts. With each package of Grape-Nuts (which contained neither grapes nor nuts) came a small pamphlet entitled "The Road to Wellville." In 1904, he marketed a breakfast cereal called Elijah's Manna. The name got him in a lot of trouble with clergymen, so he renamed it Post Toasties.

The name of Aunt Jemima pancake mix was taken from a popular song of 1889. The name of the woman pictured on the box is Nancy Green.

Trees

The cherry trees in Washington, D.C., are the gift of the mayor of Tokyo to the city of Washington. They were planted on March 27, 1912, by President Taft's wife and the wife of the Japanese ambassador.

There are 2.6 million trees in New York City; 2 million are in parks and the rest are along the streets. Their average lifespan is 7 years. (Trees in the city suffer many indignities, and it should be noted that the 1980 census found 202 families in New York City who use wood as cooking fuel.)

The bristlecone pines of California are the oldest living things on earth. Some of them are over 4,000 years old.

The world's tallest tree is a 368-foot redwood in Humbolt County, California.

Trick or Treat

The girl on the label of White Rock beverages is Psyche, the mortal princess beloved of Cupid. She has been kneeling on a rock over a pond, gazing at her reflection in the water, since 1894. When she first appeared on the labels, she was 5'4" tall, weighed 140 pounds, and had measurements of 37-27-38. On the current label, she is 5'8" tall, weighs a svelte 118 pounds, and has measurements of 35-24-34. She knelt on her rock quite topless until 1975, when the White Rock company replaced her painted image with a photograph in some of its ads. She has always had wings: in Greek, *psyche* means both "soul" and "butterfly."

Alka-Seltzer was introduced by Miles Laboratories in 1931.

Tom Carvel, famous manufacturer of ice cream, was originally a Dixieland musician.

The grinning chef on the cover of Cream of Wheat packages was a waiter in Kohlsaat's Restaurant in Chicago. His name was Rastus.

Joseph Lister, first Baron of Lister of Lyme Regis, was a great believer in Louis Pasteur's work. He studied the inflammation of wounds and established antiseptic surgical procedures. Listerine, which first appeared in 1880, is named after him.

William Wrigley manufactured soap; his son, William Wrigley, Jr., drove a wagon selling the soap door-to-door. For 10 years, young Wrigley, Jr., sold soap, and when the price of the soap was raised, he took to giving away "premiums"—little gifts—to his customers. He gave away all sorts of things, including cookbooks, chewing gum, and cologne.

He also added baking powder to his line. The preferred premium turned out to be the chewing gum, and eventually Wrigley realized that the chewing gum was more popular than the baking powder or the soap. Wrigley decided to forget about those products—hence, the Wrigley, Jr., Company, founded in 1898 and now the world's largest manufacturer of gum.

Elsie, the cow on Borden's packages, has a husband named Elmer, a daughter named Beulah, and a son named Beauregard.

The Hershey Bar was invented by Milton S. Hershey in 1894.

Henry J. Heinz already had a product line with well over 57 items—including his famous ketchup—when, one morning in 1896, he took a ride on an elevated train in New York City. The train car was full of advertisements for various products, but one of the ads struck Heinz as particularly interesting. An ad for a brand of shoes, it offered "21 styles." Heinz liked the idea of using a number, and—for reasons of his own—he liked the number 57. He quickly devised the slogan "57 Varieties." New York City's first large electric sign—6 stories high and lit with 1,200 lights—was put up on the side of a building at the corner of Fifth Avenue and 23rd Street. It was an ad for Heinz's products and included a 40-foot-long green pickle and Heinz's further-evolved slogan: "57 Good Things for the Table."

Thirty-four years after Heinz's fortuitous encounter with the shoe advertisement, James Dewar and a friend were walking along a street talking about Dewar's new product, which he called Little Short Cake Fingers. As the two men walked along, they passed a shoe factory with a sign that read, "Home of Twinkle Toe Shoes." The sign gave Dewar's friend an idea: "You might call your new baby 'Twinkle Fingers.'" Dewar thought a while and then said, "Let's call them plain 'Twinkies.'"

America's first brushless shaving cream was Burma-Shave. It got its name because its manufacturer, Clinton Odell, already had a product called Burma-Vita, a liniment containing oils from Burma. Allan Odell, son of the company's founder, came up with a bright idea for advertising the new product: a series of five-line jingles, each line painted on a sign with a sixth sign bearing the product's name, the signs placed in order, about 100 feet apart, along a highway. On September 9, 1926, the first Burma-Shave signs appeared on U.S. Highway 65 near Lakeville, Minnesota. They read: "Chear Up / Face / The war / Is Over / Burma Shave." Hundreds of Burma-Shave signs appeared on roadways across the nation. Among the most popular were "He played / A sax / Had no B.O. / But his whiskers scratched / So she let him go / Burma-Shave" and "Within this vale / Of toil and sin / Your head grows bald / But not your chin / Burma-Shave."

Smith Brothers Cough Drops were immediately popular when they first appeared—so popular that they were soon imitated. Since the drops were sold out of glass jars in stores, buyers could never be certain they were buying the genuine article. In 1872, the two brothers (William and Andrew) packed their product in paper containers, becoming the first company to distribute its ware in a factory-sealed package.

Ralston's Health Club Breakfast food went on sale in 1898. It was produced for the 800,000 members of Ralston's Health Club, an organization founded by Dr. Ralston of Baltimore.

The name of the sailor boy on the Cracker Jack box is Jack; his dog's name is Bingo.

TV Characters

Doctor Kildare practiced at Blair General Hospital. In five years on the air, young Kildare only advanced from intern to resident.

Maude, of the show of the same name, first appeared several times as Edith Bunker's cousin on *All in the Family*.

Flipper was played by Susie.

The Girl from U.N.C.L.E. was April Dancer (Stefanie Powers).

The title character of *Mr. Peepers* was Robinson J. Peepers, a science teacher at Jefferson Junior High (played by Wally Cox). His friend was English teacher Harvey "Wes" Weskitt, played by Tony Randall. Wes's fellow English teacher was Mrs. Gurney (Marion Lorne).

Original Mouseketeers were Annette Funicello, Cubby O'Brien, Cheryl Holdridge, and Karen Pendleton. *The Mickey Mouse Club* debuted in October 1955 on ABC. Jimmie Dodd was the host.

Jim Rockford's father was Joseph "Rocky" Rockford, played by Noah Beery.

Alice Kramden's (*The Honeymooners*) maiden name was Gibson. She and Ralph Kramden met while they were both working for the WPA.

Mr. Lucky, owner of the yacht *Fortuna*, was played by John Vivyan. His partner was Andamo (Ross Martin).

In *All in the Family*, Archie Bunker was a dock foreman for the Prendergast Tool and Die Company.

Jack Lemmon tried sitcom once as the star of a 1950 series called *That Wonderful Guy*, about an aspiring actor/valet named Harold. Only a few shows were broadcast.

Merv Griffin hosted three game shows: *Word for Word*, *Keep Talking*, and *Play Your Hunch*.

Sister Bertrille (Sally Field), *The Flying Nun*, was Elsie Ethrington before entering the convent.

Dan Rowan's early occupation was bartender, while Dick Martin worked as a used-car salesman.

Rin-Tin-Tin and Corporal Rusty lived at Fort Apache, California, with the 101st Cavalry, including Lt. Rip Masters and Sgt. Biff O'Hara.

Lieutenant Columbo's first name was never given.

Dale Evans's horse was named Buttercup. (Annie Oakley's horse in the *Annie Oakley* series was also named Buttercup.) Dale and Roy's ranch cook, Pat Brady, had a jeep named Nellybelle.

Peter Gunn (Craig Stevens) could often be found at Mother's Night Club, where his girl friend Edie Hart sang. And he often ran into Lt. Jacoby (Herschel Bernardi) in the course of his detective work. Edie was played by Lola Albright, who later played Constance MacKenzie on *Peyton Place*, replacing Dorothy Malone.

The ghosts on *Topper* (George and Marian Kirby) had a St. Bernard dog named Neil who drank hard liquor. They all made life difficult for Cosmo Topper, a vice president of the National Security Bank.

A good way to shorten your life was to marry Ben Cartwright. The wives of Ben on *Bonanza*, and their sons, were

Elizabeth Stoddard (mother of Adam), Inger, a Swede (mother of Eric Hoss), and Marie DeMarné (mother of Little Joe). Elizabeth died after childbirth, Inger was killed by Indians, and Marie was killed when thrown by her horse.

Sergeant Preston's horse was named Rex (*Sergeant Preston of the Yukon*).

The character played by David Carradine in *Kung Fu* was Kwai Chang Caine, a Shaolin priest. His master, Po, called him Grasshopper.

Steve Austin, *The Six Million Dollar Man*, is a cyborg—a cybernetic organism.

The stunt woman for the Bionic Woman was Rita Egleston; for Wonder Woman, Beth Nuter filled in.

The father in *Father Knows Best* was Jim Anderson, who managed the General Insurance Agency. He called his daughters Princess (Betty—Elinor Donahue) and Kitten (Kathy—Lauren Chapin); son Bud was really James, Jr.

In *Make Room for Daddy*, Danny Williams's first wife, Margaret, died and Danny married Kathleen O'Hara, a nurse who was hired to take care of son Rusty when he was sick with the measles. Kathy's daughter was Patty on ABC but changed to Linda on CBS.

The Gillis family lived at 285 Norwood Street in Central City, site of the Gillis Grocery Store. The main love interest in *The Many Loves of Dobie Gillis* (Dwayne Hickman) was Thalia Menninger (Tuesday Weld), although she had a rival in Zelda Gilroy (Sheila James), and Dobie had a rival for Thalia in Milton Armitage (Warren Beatty). Dobie's beatnik buddy was Maynard G. Krebs (Bob Denver).

Jeannie the genie (*I Dream of Jeannie*) was born in Baghdad on April 1 in 64 B.C. Jeannie was played by Barbara Eden; her astronaut-master Tony was played by Larry Hagman. Jeannie called on her magic powers by crossing her hands over her chest and blinking her eyes.

Bret and Bart Maverick had a British cousin, Beau, played by Roger Moore. They also had a father, Beauregard "Pappy" Maverick, played by James Garner.

Sanford and Son (Fred and Lamont) lived and operated their junk business at 9114 South Central in Los Angeles. Fred's dead wife, on whom he was wont to call, was Elizabeth.

Detective Sgt. Joe Friday carried badge no. 714, and he had a fiancée, Ann Baker. He went through four partners: Detective Sgt. Ben Romero, Sgt. Jacobs, Officer Frank Smith, and Officer Bill Gannon.

The Beverly Hillbillies lived at 518 Crestview Drive. The Clampett family consisted of Jed (widowed), daughter Elly May, mother-in-law Daisy "Granny" Moses, and nephew Jethro Bodine. Jed kept his money at the Commerce Bank. Elly May's first boyfriend was Dash Riprock, movie star, whose real name was Homer Noodleman.

The model on *Let's Make a Deal*, hosted by Monty Hall, was Carol Merrill.

Early stars of *Peyton Place* were Mia Farrow as Alison MacKenzie and Ryan O'Neal as Rodney Harrington, with Mariette Hartley as Clair.

Irish McCalla was Sheena, Queen of the Jungle. Her stunt person was Raul Gaona, because no stunt woman McCalla's size (6'1") could be found.

Carrie Ingalls on *Little House on the Prairie* was played by twins, Lindsay and Sidney Green Bush. The Ingalls family dog was Jack.

On TV, Flash Gordon was played by Steve Holland; the show debuted in 1953. In the movies, Larry "Buster" Crabbe portrayed Flash. Three Flash Gordon movies were made: *Flash Gordon* (1936), *Flash Gordon's Trip to Mars* (1939), and *Flash Gordon Conquers the Universe* (1940).

The host of *The Inner Sanctum*, heard but not seen, was Paul McGrath.

The hosts of *Death Valley Days*, in order, were Stanley Andrews (called the Old Ranger), Ronald Reagan, Robert Taylor, and Dale Robertson.

The Brady Bunch shared four bedrooms and two bathrooms.

Perry Mason's receptionist was Gertie Lade (Connie Cezon).

The original Three Stooges were Larry Fine, Moe Howard, and Curly Howard. Curly was replaced first by Shemp Howard, then by Joe De Rita.

In *That Girl*, Ann Marie's father was Lou Marie, who owned the La Parisienne restaurant. Ann's agent (she was an aspiring actress) was the Gilliam & Norris Theatrical Agency.

Joan's husband in *I Married Joan* was domestic-relations judge Bradley Stevens (Joan Davis and Jim Backus).

Samantha Stevens, the witch on *Bewitched*, had an identical cousin named Serena. Both were played by Elizabeth Montgomery, but the credits listed Pandora Sparks for Serena.

The Cleaver family lived at 211 Pine Street in Mayfield. Beaver's real name was Theodore. His brother Wally's girl friend was Julie Foster (played by Cheryl Holdridge).

Bob and Ray were Bob Elliott and Ray Goulding.

Howdy Doody had 72 freckles. His twin brother was Double Doody.

Regular panelists on the CBS network show *I've Got a Secret* were Steve Allen, Bill Cullen, Faye Emerson, Jayne Meadows, Henry Morgan, and Betsy Palmer.

The December Bride was Lily Ruskin (Spring Byington), a widow who lived with her daughter and son-in-law, Ruth and Matt Henshaw.

The star of *The Invisible Man*, 1958 syndicated TV series, was not identified by the show's producer.

My Friend Irma (Marie Wilson) lived at Mrs. O'Reilly's Boarding House (Apt. 3-B) in New York City. Her first roommate was Jane Stacey, who was followed by Kay Foster.

Richie Cunningham of *Happy Days* had an older brother, Chuck, played by Gavan O'Herlihy.

The Mod Squad cops all started in police work after being arrested on minor charges.

F Troop was stationed at Fort Courage, Kansas. Members of the local Hekawi Indian tribe included Wild Eagle, the chief; Papa Bear; and Roaring Chicken, the medicine man. The trooper who couldn't speak English was Private Hoffenmeuller, a German.

Patty Duke was a contestant on *The $64,000 Challenge* at

the age of 11, in 1958. She won $32,000—and was coached on the questions and answers. ("They Even Fixed the Kid" headlined the New York *Post* on November 4, 1959.)

Gabe Kotter taught his Sweathogs Special Guidance Remedial Academics at James Buchanan High School.

Ray Milland's character, drama professor Ray McNulty, taught first at Lynnhaven College (on *Meet Mr. McNulty*) and then at Comstock College (on *The Ray Milland Show*).

The title character in the series *Mama* was Marta Hansen (played by Peggy Wood). She and husband Lars (Judson Laire), a carpenter, lived in a big white house on Elm Street with their children, Nels, Katrin, and Dagmar. The series was based on a book by Kathryn Forbes called *Mama's Bank Account*. The Aldrich Family also lived on Elm Street, but in Centerville, not San Francisco.

The one-armed man, whose name was Johnson, did kill Helen Kimble on *The Fugitive*.

Chris Hale (John McIntire) replaced Seth Adams (Ward Bond) in 1961 as the wagonmaster in *Wagon Train*.

Roosevelt Grier played Gabe Cooper on *Daniel Boone*. Cooper was a runaway slave and actually Tuscarora Chief Canawahchaquaoo.

Ramar of the Jungle (White Witch Doctor) was really Dr. Thomas Reynolds, a research scientist. His assistant was Prof. Ogden.

The trail boss on *Rawhide* was Gil Favor (Eric Fleming), the trail scout was Pete Nolan (Sheb Wooley), and the cook was Wishbone (Paul Brinegar). The ramrod, Rowdy Yates, was played by Clint Eastwood.

John Beresford Tipton, *The Millionaire,* lived at Silverstone, his estate. His million-dollar checks were drawn on Gotham City Trust and Savings. Tipton's voice was Paul Frees.

Gomer Pyle's superior was Sgt. Vincent Carter. Gomer's friend Lou Anne Poovie sang at the Blue Bird Cafe.

My Favorite Martian lived on Earth as Martin O'Hara (Ray Walston), uncle of Tim O'Hara (Bill Bixby), who discovered the crashed UFO. Tim was a reporter for the Los Angeles *Sun.*

On *Wanted: Dead or Alive,* Steve McQueen played bounty hunter Josh Randall, whose firearm was a .30-40 sawed-off carbine rifle named the Mare's Laig.

Batgirl was added to the *Batman* series after questions were raised about Batman and Robin's relationship. Batgirl was Barbara Gordon, daughter of the police commissioner.

Matt Dillon's horse on *Gunsmoke* was named Marshal. The bartender at Kitty Russell's Longbranch Saloon was Sam. Doc Adams's first name was Galen. And Festus had a mule named Ruth.

Dick on *The New Dick Van Dyke Show* was Dick Preston, first a host of a variety/talk show in Phoenix, Arizona, called *The Dick Preston Show* and later an actor playing Dr. Brad Fairmont in a soap opera called *Those Who Care.*

Mr. Ed was a talking horse who would speak only to Wilbur Post (Alan Young), whose barn he lived in.

The Lone Ranger sometimes appeared without his mask—but disguised, of course. Most often he was the Old Timer. Other personas were José, a Mexican bandit; Don Pedro O'Sullivan, an oddly named Swede; and a medicine hawker, Professor Horatio Tucker.

The Monkees were Davy Jones, Mike Nesmith (with the wool hat), Mickey Dolenz, and Peter Tork.

Ozzie's occupation was never mentioned on TV's *The Adventures of Ozzie and Harriet*. The Nelson family resided at 822 Sycamore Road in Hillsdale.

My Mother the Car was Abigail Crabtree, reincarnated as a 1928 Porter, license plate PZR 317. Ann Sothern did her voice, which came from the car radio.

The original panelists on *What's My Line* (which debuted on February 2, 1950) were Dorothy Kilgallen, Arlene Francis, and Louis Untermeyer. Untermeyer was replaced by Bennett Cerf in 1952.

The three Bradley girls in *Petticoat Junction*, who helped their mother Kate run Hooterville's Shady Rest Hotel, were Billie Jo, Bobbie Jo, and Betty Jo.

Lucy and Ricky Ricardo lived at 623 East 68th Street, Apt. 4-A, in New York City. Ricky performed at the Tropicana for $150 a week; his theme song was "Ba-ba-lu." Lucy's maiden name was MacGillicuddy. Little Ricky's babysitter was upstairs neighbor Mrs. Trumbull. Lucy and Ricky (and Lucy and Desi) were married at the Byram River Beagle Club in Greenwich, Connecticut. Lucille Ball's mother attended the filming of every episode of *I Love Lucy*.

The Rebel was Johnny Yuma (Nick Adams), a former Confederate soldier.

Maxwell Smart, Agent 86, of *Get Smart* worked for C.O.N.T.R.O.L. and against K.A.O.S. His partner was Agent 99, whose real name was never mentioned.

Members of *The Real McCoys* were Grandpa Amos, Luke

and his wife Kate ("Sugar Babe"), and Luke's siblings Hassie and Little Luke. Amos ran a roadside egg business with Harry Purvis.

My Little Margie was Margie Albright, who lived with her widowed father Vern at the Carlton Arms in New York City, next door to Mrs. Odettes. The elevator was operated by Charlie. Margie's perennially broke boyfriend was Freddy Wilson. Vern had a woman friend, Roberta Townsend. He worked at Honeywell and Todd, for boss George Honeywell.

The Nurses toiled at Alden General Hospital in New York City. Liz Thorpe was played by Shirl Conway, and Gail Lucas was portrayed by Zina Bethune.

The Munsters and what they were: Herman, a Frankenstein-monster look-alike and funeral director at Gatemen, Goodbury, and Graves; Lily, a vampire; Edward Wolfgang, their son, a werewolf; Grandpa, Count Dracula; niece Marilyn, normal young girl. Their pets were Igor, a bat; Spot, a prehistoric beast; and a Poe-quoting raven.

The identical cousins portrayed by Patty Duke in *The Patty Duke Show* were Patty Lane, American, and Cathy Lane, English. Duke's stand-in to play whichever cousin Duke wasn't then playing was Rita McLaughlin.

The Rifleman (Lucas McCain/Chuck Connors) had a son, Mark, played by Johnny Crawford. Lucas was the fastest with a .44-40 rifle.

Hogan's Heroes resided in Stalag 13. Hogan's code name was Papa Bear. The French corporal in Stalag 13 was Louis LeBeau, and the English corporal was Newkirk.

In *Our Miss Brooks*, Connie Brooks's heartthrob was Philip Boynton, biology teacher, and her adversary was Osgood Conklin, principal. Her landlady was Mrs. Davis, who had a cat named Minerva.

TV Firsts

The first edition of *TV Guide* appeared on April 3, 1953.

American Bandstand aired locally in Philadelphia from 1952 to 1957 before it went national on ABC.

Search for Tomorrow and *Love of Life* both debuted on CBS-TV on September 9, 1951.

The first broadcast of the *Today Show* was on Monday, January 14, 1952. Predecessors to Barbara Walters and Jane Pauley as the "Today Girl" (her original title) included Estelle Parsons (the first one), Helen O'Connell, Betsy Palmer, Florence Henderson, and Maureen O'Sullivan. Henderson, miffed at a remark by host Dave Garroway, once picked the cushion up off her chair and whacked Garroway across the face with it—on the air.

Sesame Street first aired in November 1959 on PBS.

Star Trek debuted in September 1966 on NBC.

Father Mulcahy of *M*A*S*H* was first played by George Morgan, later by William Christopher.

Tiny Tim wed his bride, Miss Vicki, before a nationwide audience on the *Tonight Show*, December 17, 1969.

The Tonight Show had three earlier versions: *Broadway Open House*, then *Seven at Eleven*, next *The Left Over Revue*, after which it became *The Tonight Show*, with host Steve Allen.

The pilot for *Happy Days* was an episode for *Love, American Style* called "Love and the Happy Days," featuring Richie and Potsie.

TV's first sitcom was *The Goldbergs*, which debuted on January 17, 1949, on CBS. The Goldbergs (Molly and Jake, their two kids Rosalie and Sammy, and Uncle David) lived at 1030 East Tremont Avenue in Apt. 3-B, the Bronx.

Canned laughter was introduced to TV sitcoms by the *Hank McCune Show* of 1950. *Variety* commented that the "practice may have unlimited possibilities." (Maybe so, but not for *Hank McCune*—which only lasted three months.)

Superman first emerged from the comic books in the 1940s on Mutual Radio Network, voiced by Bud Collyer. This was followed by an animated movie by Paramount. Columbia made a serial in 1948. That and Columbia's feature-length film, *Atom Man vs. Superman* (1950), starred Kirk Alyn. The 1951 film *Superman and the Mole Men* starred George Reeves and was the TV pilot, in two parts (the only two-part TV episode). Noel Neill played Lois Lane in *Atom Man* and, later, in the TV series; TV's first Lois was Phyllis Coates.

The quiz show scandals began in 1957 with Herbert M. Stempel, a *Twenty-One* contestant disgruntled when the producers asked him to step aside in favor of Charles Van Doren. The New York papers couldn't confirm Stempel's story until 1958, when Eddie Hilgemeier, Jr., a *Dotto* contestant, discovered his opponent had been provided with the answers. Hilgemeier told the New York *Post* and the investigations were on.

The pilot film for *Police Woman* was "The Gamble," which was an episode of *Police Story*. In the pilot, Angie Dickinson played detective Lisa Beaumont; in the series she was Sgt. Suzanne "Pepper" Anderson.

Happy Days was a summer variety show in 1970, hosted by Louis Nye, featuring 1930s and 1940s entertainment.

The Cisco Kid was the first color television series.

The first live TV sitcom ran from 1947 to 1950 and was called *Mary Kay and Johnny*, featuring newlyweds Mary Kay and Johnny Stearns, who lived in Greenwich Village and were joined by their (real) baby, Christopher, in 1948.

The first TV commercial aired on American television was a 20-second advertisement for Bulova watches that appeared on July 1, 1941, on WNBT-NY. The ad cost the advertiser $9.

TV Shows

The General Electric College Bowl was broadcast "live from New York."

The boat that sank and marooned them all on Gilligan's Island was the chartered sightseeing boat the S.S. *Minnow.*

What are the days of our lives? "Like sands through the hour glass, so are the days of our lives."

Paladin's card read "Have Gun—Will Travel. Wire Paladin, San Francisco." Paladin was headquartered at the Hotel Carlton.

Contestants on *Truth or Consequences* had to answer a nonsense riddle before Beulah the Buzzer sounded. Hosts were Ralph Edwards, Jack Bailey, and Bob Barker.

America's favorite television show is *60 Minutes*. About the same number of men as women watch it. The second favorite? *Three's Company*, which has more female fans than male.

The Phil Silvers/Sergeant Bilko show was titled *You'll Never Get Rich* before it was syndicated. Locale was Camp Fremont, Fort Baxter, Roseville, Kansas. Commanding officer was Col. John T. (Jack) Hall. Sgt. Bilko's girl friend was Master Sgt. Joan Hogan.

The Wyatt Earp Show (full name: *The Life and Times of Wyatt Earp*) took place in two towns. It started in Dodge City, Kansas, and later moved to Tombstone, Arizona.

The bar next to 77 Sunset Strip was Dino's; its parking-lot attendant was J. R. Hale. 77's attendant was Kookie, whose full name was Gerald Lloyd Kookson III.

On TV in the Walt Disney series, Zorro had two horses: a white one named Phantom and a black one named Tornado.

Guests appearing on the opening night of *The Ed Sullivan Show*, June 20, 1948 (then called *The Toast of the Town*), were: Dean Martin and Jerry Lewis, Richard Rodgers and Oscar Hamerstein II, Lee Goodman, Jim Kirkwood, and Ruby Goldstein.

Here Comes the Bride, a 1951 DuMont network show, featured actual wedding ceremonies being performed for TV.

Tod Stiles (Martin Milner) and Buzz Murdock (George Maharis) roamed along Route 66 in a 1960 Chevrolet.

On March 16, 1966, *Gemini 8* astronauts Neil Armstrong and David Scott had to perform an emergency splashdown when their spacecraft developed a short circuit. Over 1,000 angry viewers called ABC-TV to protest the network's interruption of that night's episode of *Batman* with bulletins on the crisis.

The sponsor of TV's *Amos 'n' Andy* was Blatz Beer. The show was cancelled in 1953 because of pressure from black groups. The janitor for the Fresh-Air Taxicab Company was Lightnin' (Horace Stewart); the company's secretary was Miss Genevieve Blue (Madeline Lee).

The Life of Riley aired for one season, from 1949–50, with Jackie Gleason as Chester A. Riley. When it was revived in 1953, it starred William Bendix.

On *Adam-12*, Officer Pete Malloy's badge number was 2430, and Officer Jim Reed wore badge number 744.

The last episode of *M*A*S*H*, which aired on February

28, 1983, and ran 2½ hours, was watched by 125 million people, the largest TV audience ever. The previous most-watched show was the "Who Shot J.R." episode of *Dallas*, which had an audience of 82 million.

Pete Dixon taught American history in Room 222 of Walt Whitman High School, Los Angeles.

Daktari is Swahili for "doctor." The daktari in the TV series was Dr. Marsh Tracy.

My Friend Flicka (in Swedish *flicka* means "little girl") lived on the Goose Bar Ranch.

The *Mission: Impossible* crew was part of I.M.F., the Impossible Missions Force, an agency of the U.S. government.

The identification number of the *Enterprise* is NCC 1701.

Davy Crockett's rifle in the TV shows was named Betsy.

Zorro hit three peaks of popularity: first in 1920 with Douglas Fairbanks, Sr., next in 1940 with Tyrone Power, then again in 1958 as a Walt Disney TV series starring Guy Williams. (Williams's real name was Armand Catalano.) There was also the 1970 film, *Zorro the Gay Blade* with George Hamilton, and the 1983 TV series *Zorro and Son*. This phenomenally successful character originated in a novel by Johnston McCulley, *The Mark of Zorro*, which was written in 6 days.

Captain Video and His Video Rangers was a continuing TV serial from 1949 until 1953, when it became *The Secret Files of Captain Video* with one complete episode each week. (This ran until 1956.) Richard Coogan played Captain Video 1949–50 and Al Hodge took over through 1956.

Gale Storm followed *My Little Margie* with *Oh! Susanna* (later called *The Gale Storm Show*), in which she played Susanna Pomeroy, social director of the S.S. *Ocean Queen*. ZaSu Pitts played Nugey, Miss Nugest who ran the ship's beauty parlor.

Laugh-In regularly featured a takeoff on the Playboy Club called "The Boom Boom Room of the Chi Chi Club."

The organist for *Love of Life* is John Gart.

The headquarters of U.N.C.L.E. (the United Network Command for Law Enforcement) was the Del Florias Tailor Shop.

Space Patrol was commanded by Buzz Corey, who (with copilot Cadet Happy) piloted the spaceship *X–R–Z*.

Hopalong Cassidy and his horse, Topper, lived at the Bar 20 Ranch, Crescent City.

Contestants on *The $64,000 Question* were placed in the Revlon Isolation Booth starting with the $8,000 question. Guardian of the questions was Mr. Harrington of New York's Bankers Trust Company.

The submarine *Seaview* was the vehicle in *Voyage to the Bottom of the Sea*, commanded by Admiral Harriman Nelson.

Car 54 belonged to the 53d precinct in the Bronx, New York, and was driven by police officers Gunther Toody and Francis Muldoon.

The Robinson family was trying to get to the star Alpha Sentori in *Lost in Space*.

Video Games

The first computer game was Spacewar, created in 1962 by students and assistants at the Littauer Statistical Laboratory of Harvard, Cambridge, Massachusetts. It was played on the large, room-size computers of that time.

The person who first developed video games—played on TV screens, not computers—was Ralph Baer, of Sanders Associates in Nashua, New Hampshire, who engineered raster games in 1966–67.

The first commercial video game was Computer Space, which was introduced in 1970 by Nutting Associates, owned by Bill Nutting. The game was developed by Nolan Bushnell, who founded Atari in 1972 and hit the market with Pong. Pong was the first big video-game success. It was designed by Bushnell and Al Alcorn.

The first home electronic game system was Magnavox's Odyssey 100, introduced in 1972 to sell for $100. Displays involving more than several straight lines were provided by taping plastic overlays to the TV screen.

Pac-Man was originally called Puck-Man by its Japanese developers. *Puck* is the Japanese sound for eating something tasty. When Namco Limited sold the game to Midway, Puck was changed to Pac to avoid the obvious English rhyme.

The prototype for Asteroids was the game Cosmos, with stationary asteroids and planets.

Gunfight, one of Midway's earliest video games, was not developed by Midway. It was a product of the Taito Corporation of Japan—which also created Space Invaders.

Lonnie Cancienne of New Orleans, Louisiana, scored more than 30 million in Asteroids; he played for 2 days, being fed by friends and surrendering bonus ships for quick trips to the bathroom.

Video game fans dropped 20 billion quarters into arcade games in 1981—that's 20 billion games played—spending 75,000 people-years at the machines. That was 49% more than was spent in 1980. It amounted to 2 times the gross take for Nevada's casinos. Also in 1981, Atari reached sales of 1 million for Space Invaders home cartridges.

Predecessors of today's video game arcades were Sportlands, in and around New York. Sportlands and other "indoor amusement shops" flourished in the 1930s, when pinball became wildly popular in the United States. The first big-hit pinball games were Baffle Ball, in 1930, and Ballyhoo, in 1932.

Flippers were added to pinball machines in 1947.

One objection opponents had to pinball was that players were paid cash for high scores—pinball players were *gambling*.

The furor over video games has its parallels. In 1942, New York's City Council banned pinball machines in the metropolis. Mayor LaGuardia warned that children were stealing coins to play the games.

Wall Street

It was 33 years before the one-day drop in values of October 29, 1929, was matched by the New York Stock Exchange. Shares slid $20.8 billion in value on May 28, 1962.

The highly successful Wall Street firm of Woodhull, Claflin and Company—it racked up a profit of two-thirds of a million dollars in the three years after its founding in 1869—was established by future feminist Victoria Claflin Woodhull and her sister, Tennessee Claflin, with backing from Tennessee's lover, Commodore Cornelius Vanderbilt. Business fell off after the sisters began publicly advocating free love.

The Dow Jones Industrial Average first closed over 1,000 on November 14, 1972, at 1,003.16.

The Dow Jones reached its lowest point on July 28, 1932—41.22.

The New York Stock Exchange firm of Ira Haupt & Company was destroyed when the Allied Crude Vegetable Oil & Refining Company went bankrupt in 1963. Allied's head, Anthony De Angelis, had used oil storage tanks as collateral for credit; unfortunately, no creditors had checked the tanks—they were empty.

New York Stock Exchange values dropped by $5 billion on October 23, 1929. Commenting on Black Thursday was Thomas W. Lamont, Sr., partner in J. P. Morgan & Company: "There has been a little distress selling."

There were 20,000 suicides in 1931, far more than were supposed to have taken place just after the Crash in 1929.

The first head of the Securities and Exchange Commission, which Congress created on June 6, 1934, was Joseph P. Kennedy.

The American Stock Exchange was originally called the New York Curb Exchange because brokers would congregate on the curbs to talk business. The name was changed in 1953.

Women's Rights

Funded in 1833, Oberlin College, Oberlin, Ohio, was the first coeducational institution of higher learning in the United States. However, the curriculum for women was not the same as it was for men.

Deborah Sampson received a pension for her service in the Revolutionary War as soldier Robert Shurtleff. After her death, her husband was given a pension as a widower of a Revolutionary War veteran.

The U.S. women's rights movement was started by Lucretia Coffin Mott and Elizabeth Cady Stanton after they were barred from participating in the 1840 World's Anti-Slavery Convention in London because they were women, even though they were official delegates.

Women were allowed to practice law before the Supreme Court by virtue of an act signed on February 15, 1879, by President Rutherford B. Hayes. Belva Ann Bennett Lockwood was the first woman admitted to this practice.

The first birth-control clinic was opened in 1916 at 46 Amboy Street in the Brownsville section of Brooklyn, New York, by Margaret Sanger, Ethel Byrne (Sanger's sister), and Fania Mitchell. A consultation cost 10¢.

A statement of the rights of women was proposed for the Declaration of Independence by Abigail Adams to her husband John. She wrote, "Remember all Men would be tyrants if they could." She added, "That your Sex are Naturally Tyrannical is a Truth so thoroughly established as to admit of no dispute."

Only four female authors were quoted in the first edition of Bartlett's *Familiar Quotations* in 1855. They were Anna Letitia Barbauld, Lady Mary Wortley Montagu, Fanny Steers, and Hester L. Thrale.

The first vote cast by a female member of Congress was a vote against entering World War I, by Jeannette Rankin (R., Montana) on April 5, 1917. (She also voted against entering World War II.)

Rosalyn S. Yalow was the 1977 recipient of the Nobel Prize for medicine. As a physics major at Hunter College, she was advised upon graduating to go to work as a secretary.

The first female subcabinet member was Annette Abbott Adams, assistant attorney general under Woodrow Wilson from June 26, 1920, until August 15, 1921.

The first female minister to a foreign country was Ruth Bryan Owen, Envoy Extraordinary and Minister Plenipotentiary to Denmark and Iceland. Appointed on April 12, 1933, by F.D.R., she was William Jennings Bryan's oldest daughter.

The first civil-service exam was given in 1883. High scorer was Vassar alumna Mary F. Hoyt.

Victoria Claflin Woodhull and her sister, Tennessee Claflin, published *Woodhull and Claflin's Weekly*, a sensational journal that supported such controversial issues as free love and published the first English-language translation of *The Communist Manifesto*. On election day in 1872, Woodhull was in New York City's Ludlow Street Jail, charged with sending pornography through the mail.

The first woman to be granted the vote lived in Wyoming. As a territory in 1869, Wyoming had decided in its first legislative session to extend the vote to women. The fact that the territory allowed women to vote delayed its admission as a state for quite a while.

The only American Indian and layperson beatified by the Catholic Church is Kateri Tekakwitha, a Mohawk-Algonquin who died in 1680 and was beatified 300 years later, in 1980.

Margaret Gorman, Miss Washington, D.C., beat out 11 competitors to become the first Miss America in 1921. The Miss America contest was once won twice by the same entrant: Mary Campbell (Miss Ohio) in 1922 and 1923.

Three women have been *Time* magazine's "Man of the Year": Wallis Warfield Simpson (1936), Madam Chiang Kai-shek (1937; together with her husband), and Queen Elizabeth II (1952).

Words Cannot Describe

The French term *millionaire* was first introduced to Americans in 1843 by a journalist writing an obituary for Pierre Lorillard, the tobacco magnate. *Billionaire* followed, in 1861, used to describe John D. Rockefeller.

California blankets? Those are what hobos slept under—they're newspapers.

The name of the jackrabbit comes from "jackass rabbit"—its ears resemble those of a jackass.

The handy title *Ms.*, used for both a married or unmarried woman, was invented by Kansas newspaperman Roy F. Bailey in 1950.

During the 1820s, volunteer firemen wore buff-color overcoats. Then as now, fires attracted crowds, and those people who were great fans of fires—who followed every rushing fire truck—came to be called *buffs*. The word is now used for any fan or enthusiast.

The so-called Parsons table has nothing to do with a cleric's furniture. The table is named for the Parsons School of Design.

The poinsettia is named for Joel Roberts Poinsett, American ambassador to Mexico from 1825 to 1829.

Wyatt Earp is famous for toting around a pistol with a 12-

inch barrel. The gun was called a Buntline Special, named for Ned Buntline, the dime-novel author who gave it to Earp. Earp lost the distinctive weapon in an unfortunate accident—it fell into a river in 1901.

A stogie is called a stogie because the drivers of Cone*stoga* wagons frequently smoked small cigars.

The word *temperance* did not mean total abstinence from alcohol until the 1830s. Only those dedicated souls who signed the temperance pledge with a capital *T* for "Total" (hence the expression "teetotaler") intended to eliminate *all* booze from their lives.

In Pilgrim New England, women who reached the age of 30 unmarried were called "thornbacks."

The so-called widow's walk frequently seen atop buildings in the East has little to do with seamen's lonely wives scanning the horizon for sails. Rather, it was a form of access to the roof to put out chimney fires—houses with widow's walks have been built in thoroughly landlocked states.

Xeros is the Greek word for "dry." Xerox machines made their first appearance in 1950.

William F. Cody (Buffalo Bill) invented the term *Rough Rider*, using it to describe himself and his horseback pals. Theodore Roosevelt fell in love with the expression and used it for his cavalry during the Spanish–American War.

Originally, an "Indian giver" didn't want his own gift back—he merely wanted an equivalent gift in return.

I n 1894, Richard Felton Outcault created a cartoon strip called *Hogan's Alley*. The strip appeared in Joseph Pulitzer's New York *World* and concerned the antics of a gang of scruffy New York City street urchins. The most popular character in the group was a completely bald youth dressed in a yellow nightshirt—"The Yellow Kid." "The Yellow Kid" became so popular that William Randolph Hearst, whose New York *Journal* was the *World*'s chief rival, hired Outcault away from Pulitzer in 1896. Outcault eventually returned to the *World*, and his comings and goings made some readers dizzy. The bickering over possession of "The Yellow Kid" was only part of the circulation wars among New York's newspapers (the Spanish–American War can be attributed to Hearst's hunger for headlines). "The Yellow Kid" has given us a phrase for the kind of sensationalistic, scandal-seeking journalism practiced by Hearst and his cronies: *yellow journalism.* (Outcault later dropped *Hogan's Alley* and created a new character: "Buster Brown.")

The word *jumbo* comes from the name of Jumbo the elephant, a member of P. T. Barnum's circus from 1882 until his death in a railroad accident in 1885. Jumbo was 11′ tall at the shoulders and weighed 6.5 tons, although Barnum claimed more.

The word *bulldoze* has a regrettable etymology. *Bulldozer* originally meant a bully: the *bull* is from bullwhip, and the original phrase was *bull dose*—a dose of the bullwhip, referring to whipping blacks. *Dose of the bullwhip* became *bulldose* and finally *bulldozer,* a bully or intimidator or an earth-moving machine.

The word *blurb* was coined by Massachusetts-born humorist Gelett Burgess, the man who wrote the poem "The Purple Cow." In 1907, when he published a book entitled *Are You a Bromide?*, it was the custom to put a picture of a cute girl on the cover of every novel (presumably to boost sales). For a special edition of the book, Burgess drew a girl whom he referred to as Belinda Blurb. Her name made its way directly into the language.

285